Anonymous

Primeval man

The Origin, Declension and Restoration of the Race

Anonymous

Primeval man
The Origin, Declension and Restoration of the Race

ISBN/EAN: 9783337336509

Printed in Europe, USA, Canada, Australia, Japan

Cover: Foto ©ninafisch / pixelio.de

More available books at **www.hansebooks.com**

PRIMEVAL MAN.

THE

ORIGIN, DECLENSION, AND RESTORATION

OF THE RACE.

SPIRITUAL REVEALINGS.

"For as in Adam all die, even so in Christ shall ALL be made alive."—1 CORINTHIANS xv. 2?

"He is the propitiation for our sins: and not for ours only, but also for the sins of the whole world."—1 JOHN ii. 2.

LONDON:
JAMES BURNS, PROGRESSIVE LIBRARY,
CAMBERWELL, S.
1864.

PREFACE.

The writer of this book is well aware of the impression it must convey to ordinary readers. It is her province to write of that which does not pertain to any earth-born knowledge. She has not sought for any superhuman wisdom: the whole of its contents have been given to her in much weakness, and in entire dependence upon the power which has guided her to its completion. She is not an ordinary "medium" for abnormal effects to occur in her presence. She exercises no control over the pen when it is placed upon the paper; neither can she restrain the flow of words which then immediately become audible in her spirit-ear: the perception of her own natural thought is all the while perfectly distinct to her, and the inward dictate is likewise distinct; there is no confusion. The subjects involve the contemplation of very much that has never, at any previous period, been presented before the mind of man. Many delicate points of observation are, of necessity, alluded to; and although the prejudices of society have not been altogether disregarded, yet accommodation of expression has never been allowed to preclude the just conception, so essential to the truthful appreciation of interior verity. The writer is herself instructed through the instrumentality of the pen; for, until the words were, one by one, traced upon the page, did no such knowledge as they convey gain access to her mind. She has invariably read her manuscript in much astonishment, and has so expressed her feelings to others when speaking of, or shewing them, her closely covered sheets.

In placing her hand upon the paper with the pen prepared to write, she has never, in any instance, known what the first word would be; and after it was written did not know to what it would lead. Thus word by word has been given without any premeditation whatever. There was no need to consult the Scriptures in the selection of appropriate texts, for they came written out before she was aware of their being needed. If she did surmise that a certain subject or explanation would probably ensue, it has usually been given in a form as opposite as possible to that anticipated; and the exposition of the spiritual method of proceeding has caused the writer of it more surprise than anything else, for it did not accord with her then existing supposition; shewing that her natural mind did not in the least influence the spiritual revealment, which invariably flowed on in entire independence of her thoughts and feelings. The only conditions, however, on which a communication could ever be received were, entire dependence upon God, not desiring to receive information on one subject more than on another; the mind being perfectly calm and free from every kind of excitement. Sitting down to write under these circumstances the pen flows on, she having only to keep it upright and read the writing as it appeared under the eye.

The readers may take this statement as they each one feel inclined. Some doubting; others believing. Some may account for this phenomenon in one way, some in another way; but there it is, a phenomenon still. If there should be discovered a solution upon totally natural grounds, to the entire exclusion of the spiritual theory set up in these, and in the pages of spiritualistic works in general, still the production of this work would be none the less phenomenal.

We are, however, not on that account anxious to insist on its truth, or claim to infallibility; for, be the mode of production what it may, it is certain that the words were heard by the ear of nature, and it is the hand of dust that has written them down. Flesh is flesh, and spirit is spirit; they blend in nature, yet it is but a natural effect that can be produced. Therefore, it is our desire to caution every reader of this book that he judge of it by his own intuitive perception of what is truth; not allowing the manner of its production to have any weight in the balance of his decision upon it. Truth cannot be made more true by any amount of asseveration; neither can that which is untrue be made pure undefiled verity by the implication of a miracle in its enunciation.

The writer is well aware of the reception these statements are likely to obtain from a sceptical public; she can well imagine the scorn with which her pretension to abnormal action of either a mental or physical character will be received; but she does not blame her critics, for she is well aware that their condemnation must appear to themselves to be perfectly just,—their exposition of the "delusion,"—as it will be deemed,—perfectly satisfactory. Imagination has been at work;—strange thoughts have arisen in her mind,—the brain has been unusually excited, —and,—the writer has been so inflated by wild speculations upon mystical themes, that she has fancied herself under the influence of some supernatural power. All this, and much more, she doubts not, will be said of herself and of her book. But she is not dismayed; and why? Because she knows THE TRUTH. That it is silent,—that it cannot defend itself from unjust criticism, is no cause of alarm to her; she feels that she has nothing whatever to do with any opposition that may very possibly arise either to the statements themselves or to the mode of their production: she has but one feeling connected with the work,—that it is her duty to place it before the public. She gives forth that which has been given to her, but does not wish to be identified with it, nor to be held responsible for it. It has all come of an involuntary action on her part, save that of placing the pen upon the paper; and she is only desirous to put it forth in order that the responsibility of concealment may not abide with her. In so doing she claims justice, and true appreciation of her motives.

The spiritual revealings she has from time to time

received, have ever been tempered to the fallibility of her apprehension, which she is free to confess has sometimes failed her, leading to misconception in respect of her own states, and likewise as regarded the import of the spiritual communications that were formerly received by her. She has no desire to enter into detail in this place, but merely to explain, that the statements relative to the *natural* conception of "germ-souls" in the womb of woman, has cast a ray of light over very much that was *deeply mysterious* to her. She had been informed that, in the course of time, a work would be written through her hand, embodying expositions of experiences that were, at the period of their occurrence, wholly inexplicable. The promised work, it was stated, would relate to the subject of "spirit-births," and would develope truth of a still more interior bearing than had hitherto gained access to her natural mind. But the fulfilment of this prediction being long delayed, she thought no more about it; and for the space of three years the spiritual communications entirely ceased. She did not believe that they would ever be renewed; neither did she desire their return; feeling perfectly content to know that she had hitherto obeyed the

Divine will in the exercise of the abnormal power, and believing it to be equally in accordance with that will that it should now be withdrawn. But at length, yielding to an impression that she should try if any latent power still existed, the writing was resumed; daily increasing in fluency and in power of expression; gradually developing into the dissertations in "Primeval Man."

The writer has not herself any intuition of the extent to which her spiritual developments may be carried; but, as they have ever been progressive, it is very possible the present work may be merely elementary to that which is to follow. She does not wish to anticipate any further revealings, or to excite expectations that may never be realized. This hint is however given, as being in accordance with private intimation received in the fulness of her mediatorial capacity.

Should any other writer, normal or otherwise, recognize the shadow of his own thoughts herein vested with substantiality, such a fact need not occasion surprise, or give rise to censure, for it is simply the consequence of those thoughts being illumined by the sun of heaven, causing them to be indelibly impressed upon every supernaturally directed mind. The present writer is well aware that luminous approximations to the revealings contained in this, as well as in her former works, have been penned by authors of more or less spiritual receptivity, both ancient and modern; but not until *after* her own mind had been spiritually instructed in such matters, had she any knowledge of that fact; causing her to note it with much astonishment.

These writings were not commenced with any intention of making a book, or of meeting the public eye in any form whatever. They came by simply placing the pen upon paper to see if her hand would write independently of volition. Passage followed passage: messages of recognition and affection from a beloved departed brother, were slowly and methodically spelt out; and it was not until many such fragments had accumulated, that any spiritual revealings began to appear. At length the whole became rather a voluminous manuscript; and, as the subjects treated of increased in interest and in importance, it became evident that they were intended by the unseen author for general perusal. With this conviction on her mind the writer prepared her work, by removing that portion of it which related merely to her own individual states, and private communion, and commenced placing the various papers in the order in which she now presents them. She has thereby performed that which she believes to be a sacred duty, both as regards God and man. The love of God promotes the love of man; therefore she prays there may be found something in this book worthy of observation in the present perplexed state of the religious world, when many are speaking but few understood. The Holy records are set at nought, and revelation is tottering at the foundation: but it is not a true foundation that can ever be shaken: it is not the rock on which revelation must ever rest, if any stone of it can ever be moved from its adhesion to another stone. We come to consolidate faith in revelation *as it stands*, not to substitute any other in its place. We come to show that the Scriptures are a house built upon a rock, which the winds and the waves of nature will vainly essay to despoil; for they are not resting upon any sandy foundation.

This work is not of the world,—it has no mortal author; its writer is herself but one of its readers; has carefully and impartially studied it; she has not, in any instance, received its teachings as truth, till her own individual judgment approved them as such; and she enforces their acceptance on none; urging no argument in their behalf. She merely places in the hands of others that which has been,—she knows not how,—unexpectedly placed in hers. Freely she has received, freely she gives.

PRIMEVAL MAN.

SPIRITUAL REVEALINGS.

The present series of writings is produced in accordance with a law to which the human mind is subject, in conjunction with that of ordinary natural law. Natural spirits are ever on the wing to earth, that is, they are ever with their earthly relatives. But spiritual spirits,—if we may be allowed the expression,—are never seen or heard, neither do they perform any natural act. Now in this statement division of principle is implied; but there is division of natural and spiritual principle in every human mind; so that we here assume no unusual hypothesis.

The possible intercourse between spirits and men is not denied. The strokes by means of which the formation of these letters is effected, are not more completely identified with the letters, than is the operation of spirit upon matter, but not in the like natural degree. There is a combination of force necessary to the production of action, and if the action be wholly referable to nature, the entire forces employed are natural powers: but if the action be of a spiritual character involving a demonstration of effect that is not in any way connected with or referable to mundane matters, then it may be known that a true spiritual manifestation has taken place.

I will shew that I was always a spirit, even while in the flesh of nature. The medium is likewise a spirit, at this present; our spirits are now in conscious communion, but formerly they were in unconscious communion. Now, we see that death has only changed the plane of operation. This is the case with all departed beings: they change their position in regard to their former mortal companions, but are not thereby enabled to disclose any truth not known to them when they were in the world; but they can open the spiritual faculty of reception in the mortal that is connected with their own spiritual faculty; and that, in consequence of the existing sympathy which causes a similarity of effect to occur in one as in the other. These things are now revealed by means of that interior sympathy which subsists between my spirit and that of the scribe. It is in *appearance* only that I am telling her these things; they are evolving from *her own* individual mind; and as a consequence of the reciprocity of action that is going on between my mind and hers, the ideas thereby engendered fall into words with which her natural mind is stored.

Lest this should fail to be understood, I will use other phraseology. The Lord is opening the interior and dormant powers of my mind to the reception of new revelations of Himself; this is the case with every departed human spirit. But I am in close approximation to the spiritual mind of the writer; therefore she is partially aroused by the work going on in my own soul. I am in her natural life as it is connected with her spiritual life: it is *thus* I am in nature and *no otherwise*. I am in that *spirit of natural life* by which all her acts are governed; and I go forward with the work, giving her impressions from my own mind as I receive them myself in the spiritual degree: she receives them in her spiritual degree, and they immediately descend into the *natural* mind, and the hand writes them down without any previous reflection being possible or needed.

The voice that utters the inward dictate is that of her own spirit: it is her *inward* soul-spirit alone that does so. The natural mind remains passive; she does not seek communion with spirits, or ask questions, however relative to the work in hand, but adheres to the heavenly adage, "Let a people seek unto their God:" neither does she desire that God should bless her in one way more than in another; she does not even *hope* that such or such things may be given her to write about. She says, "If it be the will of God that I should know anything, He will certainly give me the knowledge of it; and I am not able to know whether it be good either for myself or others." Then is she instructed in that which is good; and that which is not of present utility is kept in the storehouse of the soul.

It is not my part to interfere with that inward consciousness which is in the hands of God alone, using it for His own divine purpose; but I am in connection with that inner spirit, and so I can contribute to its openness to the divine voice: the conjunction of spiritual with natural law is thus substantiated.

The law of unconscious spiritual action is not, at this day, in the least understood. It is supposed that no effect can possibly occur without mental consciousness; whereas the truth is, that no *real* spirit manifestation can, by any means, take place unless the spirit so employed can be sustained in unconsciousness, in so far as the *natural* manifestation is concerned: for, if he were to know and feel that he is acting in the production of effects which do not pertain to his own sphere, he would become a subject of the sphere he has for ever left. Consciousness is identical with presence: if I am enabled to act independently of all mortal conditions, then I am not disturbed by any pre-existing states which have all passed, even from my memory. I go on with my own spiritual work, that of impressing upon my own mind the new facts and the new knowledges, which I find are to be obtained in the present phase of my life. I have no ground for speculation, for all is to my perception clear; no cloud ever veils the light of my life; and, as I am *interiorly* beloved and *interiorly* love in return, so all my spirit perceptions transplant themselves into the mind of the scribe; she thinking naturally, believes that I am explaining certain mysteries which are known to myself, being in a condition to do so. But, the truth is, she is herself drawing it all forth out of my mind: I am thus unconsciously acted upon. I cannot control the flow of my own thought any more than she can hers, and we are in simultaneous action: but I do not think in words as she does. The idea is present to my mind that spirits are in that respect different to mortals, that thought goes into her brain, falls into her language, and the result is inevitable; the present writing is set in motion, not one word of which has been evolved from any previous reflection on either part.

These particular statements are made in accordance with the same law as any other portion of these abnormal writings; and if any should conceive that such an act is derogatory to the professed spiritual origin of the work, they are herein given to know that it is so done by means of an unconscious mental action on the part of the scribe as well as on that of the spiritual agent; for unless her mind can be controlled to work in unconsciousness, it cannot effect the present proceeding. I am in her life, or rather conversant with her mental temperament; and my disembodied mind is as much affected by her sphere as her embodied mind is by mine. There is a complete reciprocity of action established between us.

I have said that I thus act upon her in unconsciousness; and yet I am found to descant upon that very act which I assert to be thus unconsciously performed, and hereby is much perplexity occasioned. The truth is that I am not more or less unconscious than is the scribe herself, who is perfectly oblivious to the mode of reasoning employed. She is thus acting an unconscious part, just as a person in a deep sleep will sometimes speak, sing, rise from the bed, and perform a variety of actions just as if they were wide awake; the consciousness being all the while in a profound slumber. The somnambulist may be questioned, and he will give perfectly correct and intelligent replies: and on awakening from this state, he is much astonished at the account given him by the spectators of his unconscious acts.

The privilege to sustain open relations with spiritual beings is not uncommon; there are those who hold intimate converse with the denizens of the spirit-world, but they do so in complete ignorance of the laws by which such intercourse is governed. The whole fabric of spirit manifestation is standing upon a false foundation; mankind are thereby more perplexed than enlightened: false lights are illuminating the darkness with an ignis-fatuus glare that will inevitably lead men astray from the path of truth into which they are seeking to be guided.

The whole machinery of spirit-manifestation is in

the hand of man: if he be an inexperienced or an unskilful workman, the machine will not only work imperfectly, but it will work ill, and will weave mischief. It is then the fault of man, not of spirit, that deception is found to occur. "The whole head is sick, and the whole heart faint." How then expect purity and strength in anything that man can do? Does he call down lightning from the cloud till it is sent forth from God? And yet he supposes that spirits can obey him, and come forth from the obscurity in which they are veiled, in answer to his bidding! But they do so come forth,—they do answer even to his unexpressed desire. They come at the mortal bidding; but clothed in filthy garments, as was Joshua when seen by the prophet: he stood then a spirit of nature, but that clothing will be removed and the raiment of righteousness put on.*

These things are not known in the world; hence men are deceiving themselves by appearances that do not exhibit any human spirit in a true light. The result is deception; false names are given: truth is set at nought: identity cannot be established. The fault is in man, not in the communicating spirits who are totally unconscious deceivers: they intend to speak truth, when nothing but falsehood is conveyed to the mortal mind. Yet they are not always untruthful: often they are found to give valuable advice, warning earthly friends of the approach of evil or mishap: likewise foretelling events, which have come

* Zechariah iii. 34.

to pass just as they had predicted: others have been employed in Scriptural expositions: in giving correct translations of foreign languages with which the medium was unacquainted: quoting passages from books which the eye of the writing medium had never scanned. Exhortation and prayer have not been omitted: infidels have embraced Christianity: the wavering have received confirmation in Gospel faith, the desolate comfort, the afflicted consolation. —All this, and much more, has been the result of the communion with spirits. It is not here alluded to for the purpose of provoking discussion; but simply to arrest the attention of those who have experienced the reality of such communion. The incongruity of fact which we have noticed, is to be explained in accordance with spiritual and mundane laws combined: if they act harmoniously, then will all work well, to the promotion of truth and satisfaction: but in the present disarranged state of society, the machinery is very easily put out of order, and then disorder is apparent in the result.

Look into your own hearts all ye who have dwelt with interest intent upon spirit communion, and ask yourselves what first impelled you to inquire if the dear departed one could speak with you? If the silent voice within give answer, "It was for the sake of comfort, for strength to bear the cross!" well! but from whom was that comfort—that strength demanded?—was it from God, or was it from the beloved dead? Dead indeed is the influence that can alone proceed from the naturally dead! They were all potent in life, with burning words of eloquent affection; they may have lit a torch of everlasting love within the now deserted heart; but it was then God-given as it is now, and shall be for ever. It was the flame of an immortal fire that shall never, by natural severance, be extinguished. If tears drop upon this page, wipe them not away; weep on, if it is good so to give expression to feelings too deep—too interior for words to embody: but know of a certainty, that for every tear there is a smile of joy; for every grief pang a balm; but not in mortal life. Do not cherish the idea that any spiritual *natural* presence can remove the pain of parted affection,—of lost natural sympathy; bear it with enlightened patience, knowing that it is a wound that will be left behind with the nature on which it has been inflicted.

Departed spirits, both good and bad, are in close and intimate relations with mortals, but as unconsciously so as are those who have no intercourse with the spiritual world. This law of *unconscious* spirit intercourse is universal and is never infringed. The spirit who is now making this communication is no exception to that rule, however anomalous this statement may appear. It is not for us to consult our merely natural feelings, and to bend the truth into conformity with them. If we do not love truth above everything else, either in the world or out of it, we must be content to remain the victims of error and delusion.

The immortal mind has passed out of physical states, and they can never be resumed. The betrayal of secret histories, of unknown documents being, by means of spirit intervention, made known to the clearing up of mysteries and the divulgence of truth that could by no mortal power have been effected, is not any obstacle in my path; for I see how the whole is done, from behind that veil which is so thickly spread over every mortal face. It is all and every part of it the work of nature. The departed spirits with whom all are interiorly connected have a *natural* as well as a spiritual mind; in that natural mind is chronicled every past history in which the communicating spirit had an interest: that mind is not annihilated, it is ever with those by whom it was in the world beloved. That mind tells the truthful tale; predicts events, if so allowed by God; relates particulars of mundane importance. It is by death emancipated from physical control; so it traverses space in a manner not accessible to mortals. It is the same person it was when in the flesh. It can perform wonders to which there is no limit, save by the intervention of Almighty power. But the *spiritual* mind is as distinct as it is possible to be: it is not conscious of any one of these marvellous acts performed in nature. It is not, however, to be considered that natural minds are wandering about the world for nought; they are gaining spirituality by their association with mortals; they are living in a mental atmosphere, and can only make manifestation of presence in connection with those to whom they are attached, or to such as are in some degree of affinity with them. These spiritual natural minds are very busy at the present day; they are delivering various messages of more or less importance, and are kept in close proximity to mortals; they are communicating with their relatives and friends to the advancement of spirituality in each case. But at the same time a great deal of perplexity is occasioned by certain incongruities, false statements, and false identities which these minds are seeking to establish. Such offences must needs come: heed them not, but regard such things as a consequence of the general influence of evil which, at the present, so universally overspreads the face of society. The spirits are not responsible for these calamities; neither are mediums or any one else; it is the result of evil engendered by the fall of Adam, into which every human creature is now born; and whether he practise evil or not, the consequences of that fall are still in him, and cannot be eradicated till he is made a new creature in the Lord Christ Jesus. To Him therefore be all faces turned. He alone is able to guide into all truth, and to shew us the meaning of things that are incomprehensible to the mortal mind. Be unto Christ as children sitting at His table waiting to be fed; then will He lift up the light of His countenance upon you and will give you peace.

The physical manifestation of table-moving, rapping, drawing, writing by hand-guiding; every phase of intercourse now exciting so much attention in the world, is, without a single exception, the result of unconscious spiritual action; not exclusively cerebral, but unconsciously so on the part of spirits as well as men. The spirit is drawn into natural conditions by the influence upon his mind of a purely natural desire on the part of the persons by whom his presence is invoked. They often do so desire it for the promotion of good uses; but they do not inquire of the Highest whether it is admissible or not; they simply request that a certain departed one will now be pleased to manifest his presence to them by making a natural demonstration upon natural elements. Then they hear a loud knocking upon the table at which they are seated; the spirit so sought announces his presence, and that he is ready to reply to any interrogatories that may be put to him. He does so, perhaps, to the entire satisfaction of all present; or, he may be untruthful, making false assertions: he may be wise or simple, reverent or blasphemous; in any case, he is a perfectly unconscious agent. If he were at all conscious of the effect he is producing in and upon nature, he could immediately become visible and tangible. If I know that I once lived on the earth, I am there now; time would be enlisted into my service, and I could not be independent of its regulations. I am enunciating a hard theory for mortals to comprehend; because they are so utterly ignorant of spiritual requirements; they look at a spiritual object with the eye-glass of nature, and discuss and argue about that of which they can know nothing. They are not unmindful of spiritual and natural diversity; but do not apply that consideration in their speculations upon the unusual phenomena occurring at the present day in their midst. It is all, however, tending to the promotion of truth, and a higher philosophy than has yet set foot upon the earth. Let it go on; and take your stand, all enquiring ones, to view the machinery of nature disarranged, to suit the new-born necessities of the spirit. It is all the work of God. The simple manifestation of a "rap" upon your table is fraught with mighty import; despise it not, ye wise ones; it is the action of nature upon nature; of interior natural forces acting upon and in conjunction with exterior natural forces; it is not, properly speaking, direct spiritual action; that is only predicable of the *inner* mind of the spirit; and if you can attain to that elevation, you will receive light and knowledge into your minds unobtainable from any other source.

―――――

To suppose that it is necessary to see spirits in order to their complete identification, is a fallacy: it is the offspring of materialism, which is ever big with such spurious creations. The truth is plain and evident enough. The mind is alive, not dead, physical dissolution has emancipated it from the limitations of time and space; and it can then communicate freely with its associates; but it is not the spiritual mind that does so, unless the mind of the recipient of such abnormal intercourse be established in the *spiritual degree;* then will much preliminary preparation be experienced, as in the present instance; but if that has not occurred, the communications received from departed beings will be of an exclusively low character, and will not reach higher than the standpoint existing in the mind of the natural enquirer; the reason is, that the spirit is only able to speak to the mortal through the exercise of his *natural* faculties; no purely spiritual development having *on either side* taken place.

But in regard to the appearance of spiritual beings; there are persons who are in the daily habit of seeing them, and they always present the same aspect they did in life, with but little, if any, variation. These are mere phantoms taking shape and visibility from the brain of the spectator. But the experience connected with it is too extensive to be thus summarily dealt with. The seer of spirits will assert the reality of his vision, which in many cases includes the communion of thought and feeling. That is not denied, but is fully acknowledged as being of very possible occurrence. The natural mind of the departed always assumes the entire bodily appearance; the corporeal frame, with every individual peculiarity, is a perfect portraiture of the natural mind; and when *that mind* is again awakened from the slumber into which it falls at the death of the body, and is again drawn into active relations with other natural minds that are still in the flesh; it needs must be that it put on the whole appearance by which *that mind* was formerly identified; and the spirit *proper* being far removed from the confines of materiality, the apparition is not a reliable witness of anything that is *truly spiritual*.

The medium for the production of this work has never experienced any degree of open vision; it would be so subversive of the present proceeding that it could not be continued in connection with it. The mortal mind is ever open to deception; it enters in through the natural senses, and no gate is so accessible for its admission as that of sight. The seer reports very truly what he has seen; but if he should have any false impression resting on his mind, it rises up into the spiritual condition to which he is open, and it gives outline to illusive vision: he sees his own brain mapped out with every fancy it may contain, in the most distinct imagery. This is the solution of the mystery attaching to contradictory seership; in all cases it is to be regarded with extreme caution. Seers are also liable to a variety of painful trials that are not experienced by blind illuminati; and they are always more or less open to delusion of hearing as well as of sight. The whole kingdom of disorder is open to the seer; he is no less so to the fair side of spiritual humanity; but the admixture causes confusion.

It must, however, be observed that every illuminated disciple of Christ is equally liable to aberration, if he is not very careful to nullify the involuntary action of his natural mind; if he cannot keep guard over it, he will have all his pre-conceived heresies confirmed to him by the speech of an apparently divine voice within.

The more intimately mortals are associated with spiritual beings, the more they will learn from them; and the more frequent *our* intercourse with men, the better we shall be enabled to instruct them in the habitude of our existence. But let it not lead to the development of seership; it may be avoided by not being desired. That it does not occur in conjunction with other spiritual gifts is to be regarded as an advantage; and also an indication of the integrity of the medium who is interceding between earth and heaven.

The seers have truly seen as well as heard all they describe, but they have ruminated in space and in time, which have no part in the life of spiritual beings, who are quite independent of nature and her laws. How then can a spirit take the form of man or of woman, which is nature's covering? Let me not be misunderstood for lack of plain words. Spirits are not men and women in the debased clothing worn by them in the world; they do not partake of natural aliment, consequently they do not possess organs that can only contribute to the necessities of natural life. It is not then to be supposed that a departed spirit can be seen of mortals *as he is;* he can only be seen *as he was,* that is, by accommodation to the standard of man's perception. Immortals are as distinct from mortals as light from darkness; it is not possible for one to be seen by the other. The phantoms that have appeared in various mortal guises, are shades of departed beings who have the memory clinging to the earth. In most cases they are seen by clairvoyants in the places of their former abodes, and do not appear at any distance from them. But it is well known that voices and earthly sounds are often produced by these phantoms; this is the result of disorder in the *spirit proper,* who is reluctant to be disengaged from earthly trammels; his purification is taking place in a region into which no mortal seership can penetrate.

Not one spirit, said to be seen and conversed with by truly good and pious men, was a conscious entity. It is not possible for a mortal, under any degree of illumination whatever, to have such intercourse as that so elaborately described by modern seers; they are not in a state necessary to admit them into the presence of such renovated beings as spirits are. The statements made by seers of the past and present century, are not, in any way, to be considered as descriptions of *actual occurrences;* they are simply scenes prophetic of the reality ultimately to be established upon the earth. That day is approaching; internal states are progressing; and external demonstration thereof is not wanting. Purification is taking place within the cup and platter; the outside will be cleansed at the last, but not till the pollution from within shall have brimmed over, and made that to appear worse which was already evil enough.

Seers are prophets, they have not prophesied lies; they have spoken of that which they did most truly see and hear; but their visions regarded a future, not the present age. The prophetic seers have told mankind of glories yet unborn; they have glanced into the womb that is big with future generations; and with fiery cloven tongues they have described the future prospects of the world. They have seen men noble, virtuous, and tender; they have seen wives and maidens loving, melodious, and spiritually united to their own true partners; they have seen society as it should be, not as it *is* in any sphere spiritual or natural.

The earth will undergo a complete transformation. All things will be made new: the new heavens and the new earth will be firmly established; then will former things pass away, be rolled up as a scroll. The dawn must precede the rising sun, the clouds be faintly tinged with the celestial splendour; so surely are the present revealings of spirit-speech the precursors of a day of universal peace; but the branch is not yet gathered by the prophetic dove; not yet, not yet.

The Scriptures involve a series of facts, such as the world has never yet been able to take into its confidence. The events recorded, took place in a region so spiritual, that, at the present day, it would be termed the world of spirits. That is the plane on which dwelt Abraham and Sarah, Lot and his wife, who became a pillar of salt. How can such things be? How can such things have place in nature as at present constituted? They cannot. There is no merely natural event narrated in the Scriptures; the whole, from beginning to end, is the record of spiritual events that did take place, that do take place in all the spiritual regions of the universe. Moses and Aaron were the Lord's ministers; they are so still: they are ministering to the necessities of the people who require the law to be carried out to the last letter—and they are in the tabernacle, in the tent of assembly as of old: the sacrifice is slain, the burnt-offering made, the sweet savour is still going up into the nostrils of God most high. But, where? How? These words shall be answered. The whole tenor of Scripture is involved in the answer, which it will require many words to elucidate in an intelligible manner.

The Jewish people dwelt in tents in the wilderness; but that was not their home; they were not destined ever to behold the land of promise. They were to be in nature tried and tempted before they could inherit eternal life. Temptations of a spiritual character affect the spirit spiritually during its sojourn in the flesh, and this gives the basement of the natural narrative; but the events therein recorded took place in the spirit. The identity of the various personages is not denied, all is simply transferred from matter to spirit, and it is thereby placed on a higher foundation than it has ever yet stood upon. The entire authority upon which these statements rest is referable to the mind, and if that does not assent to these explanations, then must the consideration of them be left, and no harm will ensue. That the Scripture histories are literal facts shall be established to the confirmation of wavering faith, and to the consolation of every loving and tender disciple, but *not* literal upon the earth *as at present constituted.* The earth is now dead, lying in the grave of error, from whence it shall be resuscitated—even because Christ has lain in the sepulchre, from whence He emerged in the completeness of divinity. As with Him so with man, as with Him so with the earth, for all is dependent upon Him, as shewn by the rending of rocks at His change of conditions, and as shewn by the rent veil of the sanctuary.

In guise a man, in soul the God, did Christ appear. He was Divine; His parentage infinite; His power omnipotent, yet He is the pattern of humanity, for He was a human being. The letter of Scripture is on no account to be lightly esteemed, much less set aside for any amount of spirituality whatever. It is as the human body of the Lord Christ. Had He not appeared, no knowledge of God could have been inseminated into the heart of man, for it is not brain wisdom, but heart wisdom that is inculcated by the advent of Christ.

The Lord is one Lord, and in Him is no imperfection. He is of undivided parentage, having but one Parent: this is the condition of His birth from eternity; but in time He had a maternal parent—one of the nature of Eve after the division into sex had taken place. Into this divided nature came He, the Lord Christ. He was before all time; but He came into time, and by so doing put on visibility. The Lord was subservient unto time only during His sojourn in the flesh; but He had created time with all its limitation, and He has made man to be as are the angels of God, yet unapproachable to himself, in so far as divinity must ever be in respect of humanity. The manifestation of the Lord's divinity was in the flesh; God in respect of His Divine parentage, man in respect of His birth from Mary, and like as every man is spiritual and natural, so is He Divine and natural. This is the distinction between Christ and man: He is God and man, we are spirits and men.

The Lord inherited, through the Virgin Mary, the united estate of Adam and Eve, for, having but one earthly parent, it must needs be so, humanity comprehending both masculine and feminine attributes which originally constituted the person and life of Adam. Hence the Lord Jesus is the *second Eve* as well as the "second Adam," our MOTHER as well as our Father. What, then, is the effect on our immortal spirits? The response to this question is embodied in every page of this book; that is the only answer that can at present be given to so vast an inquiry. There are, however, dependants upon the question, to which immediate attention may be paid. The whole subject of the visibility, or otherwise, of departed beings, is partially involved in every postulate laid down in this volume; and if that point is not met at the commencement, the whole will be of impossible comprehension.

Man in the *interiors* of his life is neither masculine nor feminine, but like unto the "angels of the Lord." These "men" came forth from interior into exterior conditions of life; no feminine form has ever appeared to the mortal view, as did these men of old — a clear indication that no angels exclusively feminine exist, yet all are in the *perfect* human form, that is, of equal and undivided proportion, one angel, to outward appearance masculine, but inwardly as was Adam ere Eve was severed from his side.

All women are as Eve after her severance from Adam. Previous to her entrance into life, he was perfect; after her entrance he became imperfect. Woman is, therefore, in the divided form of life as well as man, and consequently imperfect also, and until these forms can reunite, so as to be one undivided form, no perfection of state can be experienced by either the masculine or the feminine member. The declension being consequent upon the division into sex conditions, it follows that when this is abolished all things will be again "very good," and Adam will have returned to Paradise in the perfection of purity and everlasting peace. The result of a return to this order in external life would be an immediate outward manifestation of its existing internal development, and states dependent thereon. The process of restoration to the primitive Adamic state does always take place in nature, for it was there the severance occurred. The body is natural so long as the spirit is so too; but so soon as the spirit becomes spiritual it is removed from the natural frame which can then no longer contain it. This is the cause of death; it is a consequence of the unsuitability of the present form of man to contain a perfect spiritual human being. It is seen that death occurs at all stages of life; but that does not contravene the foregoing statement.

The Lord is ever desirous for the restoration of the human race to the order in which it was established from the beginning of creation, but, from which, it has declined. That Divine Will is ever active. It is not limited in its operation by any hindrance that man can set up. If God does not condemn any spirit to hell, then he does exalt it to heaven; and if He willeth so to do, He does carry out that will in all fulness.

The household of Christ is one dwelling-place. There are many paths leading to it. Some narrow, some broad; but they all lead in one direction. There is but one point of attraction—that is God. But God is not obeyed. The wicked man turneth away his heart from the love of God, and he will not obey His commands. "Touch not the unclean thing" is the cry of Omnipotence; it is the cry of God in accommodation to human weakness. If God so cries to any of us, and we will not hear—will not obey, then has God spoken in vain, and our Creator has formed us with capacities to disobey Him, tending only to accelerate our downward course, and finally to immolate our souls in eternal darkness. Believe it not. The will you are conscious of exercising is the will of God, aiding you in the work of regeneration; it is, in its love for you, working out all the interior depravity of the fallen nature which you—the wicked man—have ultimated in the flesh of nature, and if you cannot bring forth that wickedness, it will smoulder within, and the stench of its fumigation will be intolerable, and, at last, will consume your soul in a hell that will indeed be of eternal duration. But the weed is consuming itself: it is working out its own extermination; it is a vital plant now, but it is seeding itself off; and well it may, for is there any soil in which it can take permanent root? Man was created for good, not for evil. Where then shall we find room whereon to cultivate briars, thorns, thistles? Have they not always been scattering seed in the winds of heaven? but it does not find a resting-place; so it is borne up and down till it sinks to rise no more on the ocean of eternity, or it is consumed in the flame of divinity. This is the fate of evil deeds; they are born of time, with time they perish. The subject of them is an object of commiseration: he is afflicted with an evil disease, and, like the leprosy, it is distorting his human proportion. He was born of God as you and I, but he is sick with degradation and internal pollution. He has caught the disease which you and I have also taken; we have it interiorly, he has it exteriorly, and he is shewing us how hideous a malady it is. But we must be cured, even as the human beast we are so shocked to behold. Yes, we have the same need as he: we are of one and the same parentage. The gentle queenly woman, she "who will not adventure to place her foot upon the ground for delicacy," she is of one mould with the savage, whose presence would be death to her; he has drawn breath in the same divine sanctuary; she is his sister, and he is her brother; one flesh is upon both; one destiny is awaiting both; one divine parental embrace will include them both. We have been fervent on this point; let it sink down deep into every human heart. Love the wicked; shun them not, as though you would have none of such. Hug them in your spirit-arms; nurse them; weep over them, they are very precious in the sight of God. They are very sick; they have to be tortured, pity them; strengthen them if you can, and if you cannot, pray for them; bear their burdens; be very gracious unto them. Be not fearful of contamination from them; the disease from which they suffer is likewise in you, so it cannot be increased; it will be removed by the contact—it will serve as a neutralization on both sides. The Bible says God is angry with the wicked—punishes and destroys. So He does. He lifts up His mighty arm, and the wicked flee apace; but He is angry with wickedness, not with those who are suffering from it. God is love, mercy, and power. He is not a God of anger, fury, and desolation; these are seen in the extermination of evil, these are not applicable to individuals, but solely to principles; these principles are exhibited in men, therefore God is angry with them—the principles of evil; but, when those evil principles are destroyed—vanquished, then, is God angry with the beings whose misfortune it was to contain them, and give them manifestation? God is just; He is so to all. All have fallen; all shall be raised; all are His children—therefore, all have received the same capacity for elevation. God is no respecter of persons, so all stand before Him in the same degree of relationship, and the same degree of consanguinity subsists in all. There is no limit to the divine power, and, therefore, there can be no limit to the exercise of that power.

There is a remedy provided for all, all being equally diseased, and having to be born again. The little child has to be re-born; the martyr, as well as the man of sin grown old in depravity. Every child of Adam descended through the spirit spheres—materialized into nature as at present subsisting, must be born again into that nature which subsisted in Paradise.

The Lord made man in His own image, after His own likeness, consequently, he was created perfect, having every requisite to constitute him a perfect human being: he was a child of God and had no other parent. A man can inherit nothing save as it first existed in his progenitor. In the case of Adam there was no human progenitor, so that all his faculties, loves, and feelings were inherited direct from God. This fact does to the natural mind very greatly increase the difficulty of comprehending the origin of evil; but, to my spiritual perception all is clear: the effort to make it so to the natural as well as to the spiritual mind shall now be made.

The will of man is ever acted upon by the will of God: it can never be emancipated from the divine control: it may appear to act with entire hostility to that will, but it is, nevertheless, one and the same will. It is God's breath that we all breathe; it is His life that we all receive, and it is not possible for that breath to become poison to us,—engendering deformity in the *inward* part; though it does so in the *outward*. To the man of sin this breath is pure—as pure, as holy, as divine for him as for the greatest saint the world has ever seen. But the man of sin is an *external* Adam; the saint is an *internal* Adam. Reverse conditions, and the saint becomes the sinner. In this view we behold all men as standing upon the same platform: none is higher or lower than another; but the evil as well as the good are equal in the sight of God; He prefers not one to another; He loves not one more than another. The good and the bad stand before Him as ONE ADAM.

If I am allowed to follow out my own course independent of the mental influence of the scribe, I shall be enabled to shew that man is a subject for the spirit of God to act upon, only as he is in freedom of choice; and that the fact of his so frequently preferring to take of the evil and reject the good, is no indication of divine imperfection in His creation; but that, on the contrary, it is a proof of the divine omnipotence.

The mind of man, unassisted by a power above Nature, can never even reflect on a supersensuous theme; but the amount of divine influx received, is determined by the extent to which it can be applied for good. If the mind were to be elevated into a region of thought above what is requisite for improvement of life, injury would accrue; and this is never permitted in the councils of Omnipotence; but the line is drawn with mathematical precision in the working out of the problem of man's destiny.

The Lord is MAN in every sense of that term: the first perfect man—Jesus Christ, dwelling with the Father in the glory which was before the world. This is the obvious meaning of those words, "Before Abraham was I am." Father and Son in God are not distinct in the sense of one being superior and the other inferior. There was no distinction of attributes. The idea that Christ is God, does not exclude that of His being Man as well; and to be God and Man, He must needs be the first Man, that is Adam. This is our Lord Jesus Christ, our Father and also our Brother; we are all the offspring of Christ as well as of fallen Adam. The spirit of *primeval* Adam is Christ;—that Christ-spirit was embodied in Adam ere he fell: *then* it withdrew into the recesses of its own divinity, from whence it could and did commune with the debased soul of Adam. It walked in the garden of his mind. Christ had formed but one personality with him; now He could only meet him on the *natural*, not on the former internal plane of life. This is the true view of Adam and of Christ; and this is why He is called the "second Adam." He is both first and second. But men's minds are obtuse, and therefore such thoughts are too high for them. Nevertheless it is the truth.

Ere Adam fell there was no outward personation of Christ: *after* his fall came Christ the Lord God and walked in the garden. Previous to the fall, Christ was manifest in Adam: after the fall, Christ appeared in a separate individuality. The natural mind of man is the Adam who was placed in the garden of Eden; the spiritual mind is the Adam who dwelt in Paradise before the fall. But, the men of to-day do not know what Christ was, nor on what plane of life He dwelt. They are thus imaged in the Adam of Eden; for he thought that the Lord Christ was without him, in the garden; whereas He was as much within him then as He was before the fall. But, I say not now how that was: my present object is to open the conception of Christ being both Man and God even previous to His incarnation.

The first advent of Christ was His appearing to Adam as a Saviour from sin; not as an exemplar, but as a clother of the naked. When Adam had sinned,—had discovered that he was naked in conquence of so sinning, then came forth Christ, and walked in the garden where Adam and Eve were hiding themselves from His holy presence. The garden was a mental condition into which this *younger* brother had strayed. The Lord God in form a Man, in voice, in demeanor, in condescension a fellow-subject, had not previously appeared to Adam: but, so soon as the sense of nakedness affected him, then arose a sense of the divine presence in his soul—in his garden, for he knew that God was present, and could see him: before he heard the voice calling unto him, he knew that it would so call, and that he and his wife would have to come forth and stand before that Almighty one; and he knew that it needed not words to tell that something had been done which ought not to have been done. But Adam said, "We saw that we were naked, and we were ashamed." They were not at all ashamed of being in divided bodies, but they were so of being in naked bodies. Had they remained in their primeval perfection, they would have been in ONE body-Adam, and it would have had no other clothing than that God had created it with. But they had been severed, and yet not ashamed. Eve had been *in* the life of Adam—she had been one with him; they were then not man and woman, but MAN. The declension was fully consummated when man took food and ate from her hand. His life had previously been nourished from within, now it was so from without: and the consequence was that their eyes opened upon a new life—a new world.

Woman is co-existent with man, they are of one mould; he is her twin brother; for they were one thought in the mind of God,—one birth from Him. They lived in His house as His child; they left that house; have dwelt in the spirit spheres, and have descended into natural life. God does not think as men do; the divine thought is immediately prolific. There is no finite comprehension so exalted as to reach this altitude, unless it be elevated into it by a reversal of the ordinary process of attaining knowledge. The mind that would be as God, to know good and evil, must not eat of the tree of the knowledge of good and evil given to it by that principle of will called Eve. But, before Eve is named or seen of man, being wholly contained in the interiors of his life; then may she give him to eat, and he shall live for ever.

But we now see that Jesus Christ being the firstborn of God, the labor of love is fallen upon Him, and upon His shoulder is the burden of Adam's fall. The mortal mind must needs be very limited in its capacity, for, it is short of its original proportion of attributes. The spirit is in the body, but it does not act as it would do, were it emancipated from that body; it is controlled, hampered in all its movements, and in its elevated aspirations, by the flesh clothing. But this should not be; the spirit should be as free in the body as out of it; and was so, ere the division of principles into sex conditions took place. Therefore, it is a disorder and must be rectified; change must pass upon man and upon woman; they must re-unite, and then will all things become again "very good." The fault is not *now* in man or in woman; for they cannot be other than they are, nor act other than they do. But the inward life is still in them both; they are each an Adam, man has woman interiorly, woman has man interiorly. This view does not, however, exclude the conjunction of man and woman as outwardly developed; when truly married they are one. That is, the inward Eve-principle of the man is embodied in the person of the wife; and the inward Adam-principle of the woman is embodied in the person of the husband, and both are inwardly as well as outwardly conjoined;

they form ONE ADAM,—MAN. In the case of uncongenial marriage-union the tie is merely natural, and at the death of either partner, it will be annulled; they will never meet again; the man will then find his true Eve within himself, and likewise the woman her true Adam, and the return to primeval life will restore all lost conditions of purity and unity of attribute in each.

The inward declension of Adam is not referred to in the sacred text, but it may be gathered by implication; it results from the act of infringement of the divine command to be fruitful, multiply, replenish the earth, and subdue it. Man should have subdued nature, but as it was, he allowed nature to subdue him: he removed his eyes from the face of God, and set them upon that of Nature; for this he was, and ever is a responsible delinquent. But there being no indication of any declension previous to that of Eve presenting Adam with the forbidden fruit, it is not to be thus lightly passed over.

The beginning of all things is with God: man can therefore only receive the end of that beginning; for if he could look into and receive a knowledge of primary causes, he would be as God—knowing good and evil; therefore man is under subjection to mortal sense: he cannot receive into his mind any truth save through the medium of his senses. Thus we see that as Nature is not able to look into the beginning of all things, so we cannot see into the beginning of Adam's declension; for it is with God alone. It were like unto a man trying to fathom his own thoughts to find out their source and origin, till at last he might imagine that he could create himself, and become God. Such phantasy is Lucifer; that is the name of this prince of the air, or of nature unassisted by a divine sanction, adventuring up to the throne of God. The Bible is a natural record of spiritual facts. Spirit must be based upon nature; and in no instance throughout Scripture is it otherwise. Thus, the man Adam was put into a "deep sleep." This does not mean that he fell asleep in the sense of natural repose; neither that he fell into a trance, or became otherwise unconscious; but it means to indicate that his life was at an end in one sphere: and when he awoke, it opened into another sphere in which life-conditions were altered. This is but the first instance of scriptural interpretation: but it will give an idea as to how the Bible should be regarded,—not as a mere history of literal facts, of times and seasons, but of states through which the human mind has passed or may pass. Mortal comprehension is deficient, not the history, which is a record in the only language accessible to mankind of events that did truly transpire; but not upon the earth as at present constituted. It does not mean to imply that any garden of Eden ever did or ever can exist in, or upon this mortal plane of life. When Adam and Eve were sent forth of Eden, they first entered upon earthly conditions. That Eden life is, however, one with the present life; it is the soul of it, and being so, it must needs find expression in the language of nature; though not in its fulness, not in every interior detail: neither is *every* Adam upon the earth's surface aware of the existence even of such a history. The unenlightened heathen, the wild Indian, the self-torturing savage, the simple inhabitants of the Polar regions, these are not aware of the record of such events being extant in any region: yet, it is a history relating to their birth from their divine Parent, their declension and provision for their restoration to Adamic glory and primitive perfection, equally so as with every sage in existence. This may indicate to us that it is not a necessity of salvation that we should know the Bible history; but it is not possible for any being carrying the head erect, to walk upon this plane of life independent of its spiritual influence. It may not appear how that can be: it is because nature is defective, and cannot extend her vision beyond the surface; she cannot penetrate the veil that sex-division has placed upon her face. This is hallowed ground, and hence it behoves us to be careful of our steps, that they stray not into still forbidden paths. But of this we must judge by the effect; if holiness be not in us, we cannot go forward; if it is in us, we may do so without fear; for God is then leading us on, and whither He will lead our willing feet we know not, neither may we stay to enquire.

The Bible history is now in process of enactment; man is coming forth of God; is descending into Eden; is being placed there by God; is declining in the interiors of his spirit; is undergoing Eve-severance; is partaking of forbidden fruit given to him by her; she is, at this moment, listening to the beguiling speech of the serpent. Every incident of the narrative is *now* in process of enactment. If it could be stayed for one second, no infant could appear upon the earth. All has passed upon you and me. The unborn babe is coming forth by the same route we have traversed.

We have seen that man is man, because God is man, but we find no prototype of any animal; nevertheless they were all created—made by God. For what purpose were they brought to the view of Adam? They were effigies of his inward principles; the outspoken word of natural life, belonging to him as a principle of adult life coming forth into activity. Man is not aware of the previous conditions of his life, nor of the extent of his infolded capacities; neither is he so of the estate from which he has fallen: for, to suppose that Adam was a man such as the present, is to admit of no degree of likeness to

God whatever. Moreover, it is to deny the Scripture, which is as explicit on this head, as it is possible to be. The Lord took woman out of man; and that is the clear meaning of removing one of his ribs, and closing up the flesh of his side. It is to be understood as a history of spiritual, not natural fact. Spiritual facts will of course engender natural facts, and then the whole narration will, as an inevitable consequence, fall into the form in which we find the subject delineated in the beginning of Genesis. But when it is understood to be of spiritual, not natural import, then we see that the one corresponds and unites with the other, together forming a complete whole.

So, now we view the circumstance of God's bringing animals to be named by the man, in a very different light to that in which it is seen by the mere literalist. He is looking on the reflection only of that which we now behold in the full illumination of the spirit. The animals brought to Adam were his own propensities which God had created, but which he had not previously recognized as independent entities. Adam had lived in the bosom of his divine Creator, and he did not know that a discreted existence was possible; he had to be shewn that it was so; he had thought and exercised his feelings and affections, in the divine sanctuary; but now they had to be identified with himself; and disunity from the divine Parent, must become a conscious perception to Adam. Then it was that the Lord

God brought the beasts of the field and the fowl of the air, and presented them all to the man to see what he would call them; and whatever name he pronounced upon any of them, that was the name thereof. Now this is manifestly a spiritual narration, taking form in nature. The variety of species observable in the inferior creation, shews that the characteristics of each kind is found to exist in man, with every possible diversity of expression. In this view, we see that the name given to each animal by Adam, indicates a distinctive quality identical with a feeling in his own breast, and that all the inward propensities of his heart, and powers of mind with which God had endowed him, were thus outwardly developed. This was the first declension from the centre of divinity; it was, nevertheless, inevitable; for, if man had always continued in the arms of God, he would have remained as a child, and never become a man. The change from childhood to manhood is gradual and imperceptible, but it is not the less decided; it is for no man to say at what point of his life it was fully consummated; it is a very decided change: and yet the life of the man is in the child, and it must come forth. It is not only a mental change that passes upon the human subject, but it is also a very considerable physical development which is then experienced. The ultimation of manly feeling produces a degree of physical alteration in the system, that is not comparable to any change that can supervene in after-life. A state of life is entered upon, of which the child had previously no experience, and no knowledge. Thus Adam was a child of God, but we are sons of God. He was a child in his sense of dependence upon God—his Father, but he became a man; yet, as he owed his life to God, he could never attain to entire independence of Him. Time is only referable to finitude, not, in any sense, to infinitude. Man was discreted from God, so far as himself was concerned; not so as referable to God. Therefore man is of low estate to himself, but to God he is still in the *primitive* order of his creation; he has never left it; it is not possible that he should do so, for, he is born into the image and likeness of Deity. The cause of disorder is in the finitude of man.

The severance of woman from man did not take place upon the earth, but on the spiritual plane of life to which all are brought previous to their entrance into nature, as the term is popularly understood. This rending of the "rib" out of Adam's body is not then a *natural* rending, but a spiritual one, and the flesh of Adam is again closed up, that is, restored to its original order of completion. The groan of pain did not escape from him in the operation of withdrawing the rib, shewing that it could not have taken place in any degree of natural consciousness. It was, however, not the less productive of natural result; for, unless this process pass upon every individual, they would enter into the present life whole Adams—undivided men and women: for they are one and all born perfect from their divine Parent, but not retaining their primitive integrity, the feminine principle is abstracted, or, in scripture phraseology, the "rib" is taken out of Adam by the Lord God, and the separate form of woman constructed from it. This "rib" being a portion of the original body of man, proves that he can never be a perfect human being, till it is again restored to its place in his physical frame: and it is evident, that no such restoration of parts can be effected in nature, *as at present constituted.* But, as it was in nature that this severance did occur, so in that *same degree* of natural life, shall the restoration of the abstracted "rib" take place.

The literal history of this transaction, does not give to the outward senses any tangible or comprehensible idea. But it was not intended to be other than it is. This present revealment is not given to supply any deficiency in the sacred text; that is neither more nor less than God ordained it should be. But the day has now dawned, when supersensual knowledge may be given to the discerning minds of men.

The man Adam had no child before Eve came forth. That outbirth was the *first* fulfilment of the command, "Be fruitful, multiply, and replenish the earth." The declension consisted in the manner in which it was obeyed. But the Lord did it for Adam, he did not do it of himself. The Lord induced upon him a sleep; then He took out one of his ribs, closed up the flesh, and of the abstracted rib He made a woman. But Adam did not contribute to the formation of this woman; he had no part whatever in the proceeding; it was effected during his sleep, or state of unconsciousness. Hence we perceive the difference between the birth of Eve and that of a child; the manner of it is productive of vast speculation, and the object of it does not in the least appear; for it is indicated, that man could have produced offspring, without the external concurrence of woman; and he would then have done so, even as God had begotten him. But the object of this thing shall now be brought to light.

The masculine and feminine principles must be correlative in order to produce effects, either in spirit or in nature; and when the fall or decline from the godlike condition began to work, then the inequality of the principles began to be observable, and a division of parts became an inevitable consequence. The Lord then saw that it was not good for man to dwell alone, and therefore He provided a remedy, that so man should not be responsible for the consequences of that which He Himself would effect, during the human unconsciousness. Now, had the declension of Adam not supervened upon his creation, he would have needed no helpmeet, for he would have generated offspring just as God does to this day generate men; and they are one and all brought forth into the image and likeness of their divine Progenitor: but they decline, consequently they must go through the like process of separation and sexual division as Adam; and to avoid the responsibility of such disorder lying with man, the Lord Himself does it in the unconsciousness of recently developed spirit life. This operation being involuntary on the part of man, he cannot be answerable for any of the attendant results, which are seen to vary in every individual case; some not manifesting the grosser evils arising from the fall; whilst others do so; making it appear as though some had been unequally dealt with at the hands of the divine Parent of all. But such is not the case; all are alike under the condemnation of sin, and equal provision has been made for all.

The life of man should have been but one life, not divided into lives; each one should have remained in the individual unity of his original formation, even as Adam is named as one man: he was a universe in epitome. God desired to make *man*; that man is now divided into every class and tribe, kingdom and nation that covers the earth: and not the earth only, but every remote sphere of human existence. It is division of one life; and the several distinct consciousnesses are all one. Hence proceeds the law of sympathy.

The Lord in the interiors of His own personality

made woman, and brought her unto the man to see what he would call her, and the name that he pronounced upon her that was her name. It was not a mere cognomen that Adam gave to woman, it was the pronouncement of her birth from himself. It gave significance to that birth; it indicated its nature and object; it spoke forth the mission of woman to be accomplished in ages, by all classes, tribes, and nations, extending over the entire range of feminine humanity. Was woman so spoken forth of Adam, or of God? Was she made merely of dust—flesh and bone—or was she a spirit sent forth from the spirit of the living God? Was she not both? God spoke forth the spirit; man the body; man the natural life; God the spiritual life. Man spoke because God spoke. Man knew that she should be called "woman," because God had indicated to him her attributes and her mission.

Thus it was that God created woman, not only *in* man, but He also created her *out* of man; He took her nature out of man, and out of that natural principle God made a spiritual principle; this He did whilst Adam slept; he was not aware of the *interior* parentage of woman, neither knew he her *inward* capabilities. He awoke a *natural* man, having during the sleep of his spiritual faculties undergone a complete transformation. The helpmeet *within* him had come forth of him. The spirit of that feminine nature still remained knit with his spirit; the body was withdrawn, and into that body—that "rib," God put life and made a woman; but she was only flesh of his flesh and bone of his bone; not spirit of his spirit,—soul of his soul, as was the inward principle of femininity, which is *still* one with every man in existence, be he saint or savage. This *interior* principle of femininity cannot be severed from man; it is too closely interwoven into every fibre of his spiritual being; it is the rib which remains, forming the framework of his entire body.

The hope of mortality has been divided into two ideas, the masculine, or the nonentity of sex in God. He has not been regarded as a Mother but only as a Father, and yet all men consider Him their Parent, though in nature two persons must contribute to a birth. This is an evidence that man thinks on two separate planes; for the reflection of one thought is herein manifest in the other: the sense of requisition is not violated in the consideration that God is a Father; neither is there any question agitated on the subject of how that can be; for the inward mind is perfectly composed about it, well knowing that God does stand to us all in the united relationship of Father and Mother.

In order that this truth may be the better understood, I will be still further explicit, and will say that God is of no sex, which is clearly only a relative term indicating the division of human beings into different conditions of human life. This view is then the truth. God is a Being of equal proportions in every particular. There is not any one attribute in preponderance over another; all that pertains to Him is in perfect equality. In His divine nature is harmony; no relative position exists in Him, no principle is at variance with another, but He is an entire ONE. Man was so created; but we now take him as he is at this day, a divided being, a half representative of the divine Being; and woman, she is also a half representative of her divine Parent. But the affections are extant in both halves, and the intellect is also alive in both, and all the requirements are the same, though differing so materially in physical construction and in relative effects. There is not the same diversity observable in the childhood of each as there is when either sex have attained to their majority. On this head very great stress must be laid. The man Adam is not said to have come forth from God a child; but to have been at once produced a full grown man with woman contained within him. But in all after generations man came forth a child, or at least, such is the supposition of mankind; but whether it be a true one or not we shall endeavor to make appear in the course of these pages. The childhood of man is not dwelt upon in any of the early portions of Bible history. Now, herein we find much room for speculation. The fact that Adam came forth a man and not a child, is demonstrable from his being always called a man, not even a youth or young man, but invariably "the man." How then did he first make his entry into life; by excision from his divine Parent, as did Eve from him? No! but as in nature, Jesus, by His divine will, made bread and fish; so could He, in the God sphere, make man without any preliminary conditions being requisite.

The man Adam, then, had no infancy or childhood; but when he had grievously declined, then the feminine part, being completely disunited from him, was told that she should bring forth children in pain and in sorrow. This is the first mention of or allusion to childhood. Thus we see that it is a stage of life dependent upon the fall of man from primeval conditions. No child had appeared in nature, but Adam had been, and Eve had been, yet, before their severance they were to "be fruitful and multiply." How was one being to do that? In the same manner that God had done it, for the man was in His image and likeness; therefore, it was the order into which he was created. And did he obey the injunction so imperatively given to him? I do not know whether it was obeyed or not; but I do know that God caused Adam to be divided in the midst because he fell away from the order of his creation. They were one and became two, not by any exercise of their own will in the matter. The man was not even aware that such a thing could take place, and when it was done he was evidently surprised. Eve was withdrawn from him; not as a child, however, did she come forth of him, but in a full grown and perfectly developed form. She was then presented to Adam, who said, She is of my own flesh and bone; but how did he know that, for he saw himself perfect as before? The Lord had closed up the flesh of his side. But the narration is not to be taken as expressed in its present form. The whole transaction did occur, but not on this present natural plane of life whereon no undivided Adams can appear, neither could the Lord God, as He then appeared to Adam and to Eve, who were what men would now call spiritual, not natural beings. On the plane of life indicated by Eden, the Lord can and does appear as the Lord God; there it is that *every* Adam falls asleep, and has the feminine portion of his spirit taken out of him, and presented before him in a separate human form; and it is the Lord who affects separation, in order that the act of being fruitful, multiplying and replenishing the earth may be accomplished. Eve is then the fruit which undivided Adam has to bring forth; she comes into nature, and there she is to bring forth also, but not as she was herself brought forth from the body of Adam. She must henceforth bear children whose capacity for procreation will not be developed till the course of time has passed upon them. Time is only a relative term indicating changes of state and progress to ultimate perfection. The child is the man or the woman in the preparatory stage of life. All its capacities are folded up within, to be opened out into the completeness of maturity.

The desire of woman for offspring is deeply implanted in her by her divine Parent. It is, therefore, from a united source that that love proceeds, and hence perfect images and likenesses of God are generated. This is the case with every child that opens the matrix. He or she proceeds forth from God one being, male and female in one form. The division is effected in nature, not externally to our senses, but interiorly within the circumference of those senses. Man puts on the body of flesh which he obtains from his maternal parent, and that is assimilated with the spirit which he obtains from his father; but is there no spiritual principle derivable from his mother as well? How is it that feminine children are begotten? Do they not proceed from the father just as much as do the masculine? and likewise masculine bodies are contributed by the feminine parent. This consideration should be sufficient to prove that *within*, each parent is in dual unity. The irregularity of the unions by means of which the children are begotten; the depravity of motive from which the innocent babe is engendered, together with the promiscuous order of life observable in the intercourse of the sexes, offer no hindrance. The soul-germ descends from God and germinates in nature,—interior undivided nature —it then descends to nature as exhibited on earth, and there it also germinates; seed goes forth and infants are born into divided conditions, the male part coming forth of one parentage, the female part of another, and the truth is, that whether they do ever meet in nature or not, the same result ensues, in so far as *spirit* union and consequent prolification is concerned. This is the case with all: no human being is exempt from this law of spirit attraction, union and prolification.

The same principle of humanity that is in nature at this present has ever been in nature. In the sight of God there are in reality no *divided* human beings. They are all perfect; they are all in primitive conditions: the male and the female are still one, but in externeity they are two: in mental development they are distinct; they are likewise distinct as to every physical arrangement: men are men, and women are women; and how they are ever to become united into one human being, the one within the other, does not in the least appear to the mortal mind.

The difficulty men have in the elevation of their minds above the control of space and time is only to be regarded as the consequence of natural infirmity, to be overcome as the spirit becomes invigorated by ascension to the heights of spirituality for which it is interiorly adapted. Time is said to have passed upon our Lord during His sojourn among men. But did it do so in reality? Did the natural sun rise and set for Him? Was there any night to His unlimited perception? Did any darkness obscure His divine vision? Not in the spirit. In the inward consciousness, all was present; the past was to Him as the future.

All children, at whatever age they return to spirit

life, are men and women. There are, truly, spirit babes, but *these* have never been born of mortal woman, but are in a stage of life preparatory to that birth. The departed infant is not an infant in the spirit; he, or she, has lived in God; has established primitive conditions in Him; has come forth of Him as came forth Adam in Paradise, not infantile, but perfect in all points, masculine and feminine in one personality. In that primeval region comes forth every child of God. They pass through the course of Adam,—are divided; the lapse of time being allowed to pass between the birth of one, and that of another. The mother of earth is likewise the spirit mother; she bears spirit sons—undivided Adams, who have become divided by birth into nature; she ultimates *half* souls, be they male, or be they female. The whole or undivided soul was previously born of her spirit. The form of that offspring was not as those she gives natural birth to, which is the *divided* form, not the whole in one complete and glorious proportion.

The relative position of the parents determines the sex of their offspring: if they are united in a very interior degree of affinity to God, it will be masculine; if less interiorly united, the offspring will be feminine. But as we find both sons and daughters given into the bosom of the same mother, we must infer that it is occasioned by a corresponding difference of condition in the parents which has effected these different begetments. If the seed has been sown at a season of less vernal heat, the sun of divine love has brooded over it; but it could only develope an Eve, not an Adam. The man-child is from God in a direct emanation; the woman-child is also from Him as a divine parent, but derivatively through man, as Eve from Adam. Hence the origin of the preference given, in ancient times, to male children, which is still preserved among all uncivilized nations.

Let it be supposed that a male child is born upon the earth, his feminine counterpart to be ultimated some few years later. He will be no more conscious of her presence than if he had no such counterpart; but in spirit he will be still associating with that feminine portion of his being. This female spirit is an infant; but not until she had been driven out of Paradise with Adam does she enter life an infant; sin reduces her to infantile conditions; she is born into the *interiors* of natural life as she is to appear upon its surface. Infancy is predicable of spirits *to be* born into the world, whether male or female; but *not* of any who depart out of it,—returning to their lost inheritance.

The subject must be clearly comprehended, or error will arise. The point of observation is twofold, natural and spiritual. The child is born of nature, the man is born of spirit. Spirit gives birth to spirit, nature gives birth to nature; God gives birth to both; man-Adam is born of God into adult conditions, not infantile. The child-Adam born of woman, indicates the imperfection of the race. Had there been no fall, would there then have been no children? There would then have existed no imperfectly developed human beings, which children are; but they are lovely and very attractive to mortals, and so they are to spirits; yet they are imperfect. How is that to be accounted for? By the declension: hence the love of disorder in preference to that of order. It is so worked up with our spiritual essence, that we confound the one with the other. We see that a child is innocent and irresponsible; that observation draws forth our sympathy; it is very meet that it should: but the attraction possessed by infancy is not above that standard; it is merely a natural, not a spiritual fascination, to which some minds are susceptible. The interior love we experience for childhood is the desire to promote the eternal welfare of each little dweller upon earth; and we should know that it can only be procured by a return to the primitive order of life, undivided and sinless. We should regard our children with the eye of compassion, sympathy, and affection, that is akin to the glance of the Almighty Parent.

But I will proceed to develope the course to be pursued in the descent into nature of the little Eve, who is now suppositiously nursed in spirit arms, previous to her advent on the earth where her partner has already found a resting-place. The spirit-birth has occurred; a whole Adam bearing Eve undeveloped into external form, has been born into that sphere where the division must be effected; that region is

Eden; there, a man was born of God; there, *every* man is still born of God,—of the divine communings between the masculine and feminine principles in God. There the man is placed; there he is divided; there Eve is drawn forth, and there is she retained in purity that is not ashamed, till enlightened by a false lumen; then she is ashamed of her severance from the masculine portion of her being; she is shorn of her due proportion; her throne within the soul of man is vacant. Can it remain so? Will not the very spirit of the air rush in and fill up that vacuum? It has done so, Christ has vanquished that spirit— that power of the air—of nature; He has restored woman to her birthright in the soul of man. The spirit of our theme is in heaven, the body is on earth.

Eve descends, driven forth of Eden; she finds herself in spirit-life a babe, nursed in the arms of an angelic mother, who has passed through a like experience herself. Eve is now born a babe, not a woman; that term implies one flesh with man; she is now complete in her own *separate* identity; she is imperfect in all the constituents of her sex. Such is the spirit-Eve, but she must still descend; be born of mortal parents, and graduate up to womanhood; she will then reunite with her Adam *in the spirit*. In nature she may never marry, or doing so, find not her true soul-partner. Yet she will be fruitful in the spirit, bearing children unto the Lord after the likeness of Adam; uniting the masculine and feminine principles into one personality. This is the life of man and of woman—they are divided in nature, in spirit they reunite.

The progress of the declension has occasioned such manifold disorder to arise, that very many human beings are removed to the spiritual spheres during the progressive period of infancy and childhood. This fact does not embarrass our view of the subject; it simply informs us that duration in natural life is not essential to the completeness of spiritual life. The life of a babe being imperfect, it is impossible that it can be exempt from the consequences of imperfection. It is therefore subject to disease and death. It is imperfect only in nature; it is not so in the interiors of its life; for it came forth in purity from God. It is therefore, at the death of the body, restored to its own primeval condition, and that was as Adam previous to the embodiment of Eve. But the departed child may leave its counterpart on earth. How then? It is the same as if one were unconscious of the presence of the other; yet in *interior* life they are one and the same being. This is the state of all. The body is defective; the spirit is perfect in its degree; the manifestation of life is various; the manifestation of infirmity manifold; the response of the creature to the divine voice is given in every language—every Babylonic tongue; every animal utters forth the speech it is endowed with by God. Shall man do less? Can he cry, and God not answer? Can he need, and God not supply? Let the birds of the air return the answer! The vacuum in nature must be filled, shall that of the spirit remain void?

The life of every man and woman is dependent upon their interior state; and the end in view is life of higher and higher degrees. The departure of infants is a consequence of their having ultimated all that is requisite; and, under existing conditions, prolongation of natural life would be a positive injury to them. This is the course of Providence; the disorder is met at every point, and intercepted in its downward tendency. The departed babe is closely allied to its counterpart, wherever that portion of its soul may be. The severance occurred in the region of life that is just within the veil of flesh, whereto it returns. The counterpart may remain an inhabitant of earth; the withdrawn one holds intimate relations with the one still in the flesh; union takes place; strength is regained; mental powers are unloosed; affections vibrate with essential life—life of order. The infant of a span is the *man* God gives birth to ere He parts Adam from his own flesh and bone. The reversal of sex will give the same result; it matters not whether the masculine or the feminine part be first removed; the consequences are identical. The whole range of human experience is subservient to this one end—reunion of the sexes: for it is entirely equivalent to regeneration and the restoration of mankind to primeval order and consequent purity. The lost inheritance must be restored. Retributive justice must have its due. The last farthing must be paid. Man did not separate himself from his counterpart, but God did it unto him whilst he was unconscious. Man required a helpmeet, and so God provided one for him; he did not require one at first, but God saw that it was no longer *good* for man to dwell alone.

The Lord had a divine purpose in the work He performed for Adam in the unconsciousness of his spirit. The severance of the woman from man comprehends the whole scope of redemption. The Lord, by that divine proceeding, redeemed mankind from the effects of Adam's fall. The Lord *then* laid aside his holy garment of divinity, and girded Himself with a towel, and took water to wash the feet of humanity. He took of man's estate; He made woman; He could only do so by creating her first *within*, then *without* Himself. The Lord visited man ere He was visible on earth. He lifted up fallen humanity; He brought Himself into contact with it; He took into His own Being the cause of man's *inward* declension. He made woman by severing the feminine from the masculine principles, both co-existent and originating with Himself. In this view we behold the Lord Christ as the ever-present Redeemer of mankind. He did not first become our Redeemer by allowing Himself to be born of woman; but He was so born in consequence of the *inward* redemption which He had effected for man ere man left the Eden of his primitive existence. This is Jesus: we must see Him in Eden, in the world of to-day, as well as in every stage of the earth's history. If we do not take this scope of vision, we set bounds to Omnipotence; we limit the Divine operation to space and time, seasons and epochs; but with God there is no time—no season—HE IS.

The earth is the basis of the heavens, and they cannot stand by themselves; mankind are the earth, and also the heavens. With equal propriety the plural number may be used in reference to the earth, for this globe is not the only dwelling place of man; he is an inhabitant of orbs that have not yet become known to our earth brethren. These have all but one heaven—one God is over all. These men do not know the Lord as He is known of us, for they have never heard of his flesh-advent; they have never needed it. They are born into very different conditions of life; they are not divided into male and female parts, consequently they are unfallen races, preserving their primitive integrity.

These beings are unsevered Adams, retaining the Eve-principle within their own breasts. These star-people are our brothers and sisters in one personality. They are our fellow creatures in God. Their origin is identical with our own; they came into existence at the same time, for every child born upon our planet a man is born upon every earth in the universe; not a boy or a girl infant, but an Adam, whole and entire, bearing Eve within the mental constitution, and therefore within the frame. Men do not there marry and give in marriage, they are *born* in pairs—in dual unity. They do not conceive children in pain and in iniquity, but they engender offspring in the perfection of maturity, sinless, yet possessing the tendency to sin: unfallen, yet liable to fall; masculine and feminine in one personality, yet liable to severance. These beings are just as natural human beings as those at the present day, subsisting on this globe. The truth is, that severance into male and female form is exceptional to an all but universal rule. Infancy does not exist upon any other orb, and if it were possible to introduce a planetary man into the company of infants, they would be to him objects of extreme compassion, as embodying the very essence of sin and depravity. This statement is incredible to the earth-man; he regards infants as little less than angels, and so they are, but not as seen from the standpoint from which the star-man would view them. He would but regard their diminutive proportion, their simplicity and feebleness of mind and body, as the exponents of sin, which would thus be externally portrayed to his outward vision.

Thus we see that conditions being varied, men are diverse, yet one and the same with reference to the Divine Being, who has created but one man—Adam. He is the universal man, typal both in body, soul, and spirit; and if you can receive it, all men must return to be as Adam in Paradise, previous to the fall. All the hosts of heaven were then centred in him; He was angel, spirit, and man. God is one, therefore there is no perfection of possible attainment for man but by union of attribute. As with God, so with man. All identities must culminate in one; then will mankind have attained unto that human perfection, glory and eternal blessedness, which God reserves for him in His own divine person. For this end was Adam created; and to this end he shall assuredly attain.

But nature revolts: she would fain pass eternity with angels; resuscitated devils are an abomination unto righteous human beings. Wherefore so? Shall God appoint, and shall it not be blessed? Christ says, "Come unto me, all ye that are heavy laden, and I will give you rest." Rest is unto the troubled spirit. The evil ones have been sorely troubled: an evil disease cleaveth unto them: they have, like unto Christ, borne *our* burdens, and carried *our* infirmities. They shall be cleansed, made whole of every malady; they shall live and not die, that is, when they have become righteous; evil is in the good man, and *some* good is in the bad man. The whole mass is leavened; it ferments, and the bread is good: it is the Lord's body. In that body live the evil as well as the good. Shall they not be made one in Him, without whom no man can live?

The breach shall be repaired; the dead arise; the devil become the angel: but how, no man may yet say. The opinions of mankind are diverse; they must needs be so; for division into sex-conditions causes the diversity of opinion, as well as of feeling, which subsists throughout the entire earth. But that is non-existent upon any other earth in the universe; the inhabitants of which are all agreed, and differ not on any single point.

They are of one universal mind; they are divided into personalities, but not into men and women; they are orderly representatives of their divine Progenitor.

Man upon the planets is unitary. Man upon the earth is disunited. Man is born Adam: that event includes birth upon every orb in the firmament: every inhabited particle of nebulæ receives its new-born son. God has moved in the generation of his offspring man: that movement is responded to throughout the entire region of space and time; every orb vibrates with the new-born life. An infant descends to *this* world, no matter whether male or female. Adam receives his breath of life in the universe. In one sphere he is living under different conditions to that which pertains to another: but on this earth alone does he make his appearance in the fragile and imperfect form of infancy.

We have seen that man is one, whether in unity or in division; whether masculine or feminine; whether one human entity or whether a universe be the subject of our thought: God created Adam; He made man. He is making man at this moment. There is no second of time at which human beings are not coming into existence. Hence we see that Adam is *now* coming forth of God: is *now* undergoing Eve-severance; is *now* being sent forth of Eden; is *now* giving birth to sons—to spirit-offspring born into every attribute that he has ever possessed. The sleep of Adam is a state into which every child of earth has fallen: were it otherwise, supernatural instead of natural beings would be born of woman. The duration of that sleep is co-extensive with the present life; it is the sleep of all spiritual consciousness: it is the hindrance to open communion with the beings that are ever awake: for till Eve was to be disengaged from the inward embrace of Adam, did no sleep, no state of spiritual unconsciousness visit him.

The progress of declension has induced upon man a perpetual slumber: it has likewise caused the woman to inherit the slumbrous nature, and to propagate it in her offspring. Creation slumbereth; it also groaneth for deliverance from the flesh bondage unto iniquity, —from the somnambulistic condition of human life; men cannot now feel that they were once Adams, Eve being within. The form of undivided Adam is to mankind totally incomprehensible: the mental unity is alone a comprehensive conception. It is, however, the form of God, and was imaged in nature by the primeval Adam. If man were in nature in the God-image, no disorder would be possible; he would be in the beauty of holiness and finite majesty. That such a form is inconceivable to the present race of mankind, is the consequence of their long and deep sleep. The spiritual bearing of this theme is evident.

The birth of the spirit is from woman as well as that in nature; and one is dependent upon the other, neither being independent of man. No woman can be woman without a masculine counterpart, and no woman can hold her life in God unless she be in the image and likeness of God, who is both Father and Mother to the human race. At this point we behold Adam and Eve in severance standing side by side in the garden of Eden: they have each slept, have awakened: are to be reunited, but on a different plane of life. Adam knows his wife, he does so in nature: before it was in spirit that he did so, she was within, she is now without him: she is flesh of his flesh, bone of his bone: hence she is "woman." Woman has come forth to the exterior perception of Adam: she has now to be ashamed of that appearance, for she did not previously exist in that form. She is not, however, at first at all ashamed, neither is Adam, for the perception that it was a declension that had taken place did not become manifest to them, till it led to disobedience of the commands of God; then it was, and not before, that the shame came on. The position of every man and every woman in existence is herein fully depicted. The sensitive delicacy of feeling so remarkable in the female sex, is the shame of Adam and of Eve, when they discovered that they were naked in consequence of partaking of the forbidden fruit. This very shame is resplendent with the divine effulgence; for, it is the prophecy of that return to the primitive order of life to which every child of humanity is summoned. It is the stay of humanity on which rests the perfection of the future life. The shame of Adam and of Eve cannot be removed in natural life: nature will not construct a covering sufficiently durable to meet its necessities; it cannot be removed by the fig-leaf garment from the sight of God. He is walking through the earth, and its nakedness is just as manifest to Him as if fig-leaves did not exist. Coats of skin must then be made for the man and for the woman: and they cannot make these for themselves: the Lord God must Himself prepare them, and then they must be worn so long as the cause for shame remains. The skins made by the Lord God for Adam and for Eve were such garments as men and women are now wearing,—natural flesh and bones that are placed upon the spirits of mankind. It is not possible for such garments to enter into Paradise; and when they were put on, the pair was sent forth of Eden. When it is seen that man and woman were originally one being, then it will be granted that they cannot re-enter Paradise in divided bodies: but they may and do live a limited period in that divided condition, after the earth life: that is the return to Eden.

Be it understood that I do not attempt to prove assertions, I make them for the enlightenment of the natural understanding, which must unravel them by the light of its own taper. I am exclusively employed in the transmission of interior verity: but if I were to attempt to prove it to the natural comprehension, I should be compelled to put on that coat of skin which the Lord is removing from my shoulder. It remaineth on, so long as it is needed, and when it is removed, I shall be as Adam before Eve came forth of him. The period at which Adam and Eve "were naked and were not ashamed," is that interval wherein man is a spiritual being undignified by the appellation of an angel. Angels are both masculine and feminine in one perfect form, but spirits are only in the preparatory stage of that paradisiacal life. The man knew his wife in nature, that is the first indication of the production of offspring. Cain the murderer came forth. Evil then had natural birth. Innocence followed—Abel was born, his blood is ever crying from the earth; it goes up to heaven, and God hears that cry. Woman brings forth Seth in the image and likeness of his father, Adam.

It is stated that of all the beasts of the field was none found that could be helpmeet unto Adam. But woman was then within him; the rib had not been abstracted from his side. Why did he need a helpmeet? He did so in nature, for he was a natural as well as a spiritual man, and he required an outward expression of his inward possession, and could find none. The beast of the field could not be the exponent of his spiritual affinities, but only of his natural propensities: these were efficiently represented by the animal creation. But wherefore did he need to have his spirit belongings thus outwardly represented? The whole plan of man's redemption from the curse of evil is herein made manifest. Adam must multiply seed over the face of the whole earth, or else he could not be redeemed. The mould into which every soul-germ is cast previous to its descent to the earth-life having to be thus provided, the man must be severed from the woman. This was the work of God without any co-operation on the part of man. The presentation of the animals and the birth of Eve is to a great extent co-relative; the one as well as the other is a declension epoch, and the succeeding consequences are very apparent in the Scriptural history.

Let no man say I claim too much for woman, when I affirm that she is the medium provided by God to rescue the human race from eternal perdition. This postulate must be allowed to stand where I have placed it, without any natural support, till we can construct one from the materials which we shall now proceed to collect: make special observation on my words, and fear not the result of a patient investigation into these mysteries. The life of man is in that of woman, and she holds her life in that of man, and both are one in the sight of God. This interior union must produce effects that are not visible to the eye of nature; for before nature was God was, and before mankind were in nature, they existed in the regions that are termed celestial. There they were one being, the man and the woman folded up one within the other in the true image and likeness of their divine Parent, in whose presence they perpetually dwelt. Here, in this blessed region, they became fruitful and multiplied, but not with natural seed, it was not then created; the prerequisites had not been established, and no natural creation was by man anticipated. He then wore the God-clothing, not the garment of flesh in which he now appears. What then was the nature of his offspring? They were God-like as himself. They moved in the same divine sphere; they came forth of him in his own image and likeness, needing no helpmeet but the one within. This was the fulfilment of God's command to be fruitful and multiply, and replenish the earth. The meaning of being fruitful is, that Adam should ripen seed. That fruit did ripen, did bear seed, but finally it descended in the scale of life, and germinated in natural soil. Nevertheless, the seed thus sown was of heavenly descent. It came of a celestial parentage; it retained the original germ from which alone it could receive its life and vivifying capacity. It was God-seed, angel-seed, spirit-seed; and it had become natural human-seed. This same germ of human life had produced undivided beings; it had also produced, in its descent, beings divided, the masculine from the feminine. It had been perfect, it became imperfect; it had descended in the scale of human existence, but it was the same seed that erst left the person of the Divine Being. To suppose that such a germ can ever have the power to destroy itself, is to admit a principle of death in God which is revolting to the perceptions of every rightly constituted mind.

The main spring of every action being WILL, it is desirable to regulate it in accord with the will of God, otherwise false action is the inevitable consequence, and if one false step be taken, the whole course of progress is thereby deranged.

The birth of woman is the result of the separation of Adam's will from that of God. Previous to the birth of woman man was one with his Creator, but he could not long maintain that holy union; the will of his human nature took human shape and form, the prevalence of disorder immediately became apparent. This is the case with every man at the present day; he is not good because he is not in the conditions of his birth from God; he is no longer one with his Creator; when he is restored to that primeval estate, he has no will to sin, no inclination towards it; it is then hateful and obnoxious to him. That it is ever so to the good man is a consequence of the *interior* union of his soul with woman; if there be no interior union, he will be an exhibitor of every evil human nature is capable of, and he is in the love of it,—it is his life, an essential of his existence. But, that he may be changed—reborn, his feminine principle is withheld from ultimation into nature: it is not born into the world, but is reserved in order that after death a union may be consummated, such as will restore the soul to the lost estate of primeval Adam.

But these truths have never yet been enunciated, and many are wandering in obscurity and error for the need of such knowledge. Mortals are not able to receive much spiritual nourishment at a time, consequently, the difficulty is great in affording them that insight into these mysteries which is so necessary for their complete enlightenment. Patience must therefore be granted in order to the furtherance of this work, and it is with extreme caution that it must be proceeded with, for, owing to the extensive prevalence of error and false feeling, much misunderstanding may unavoidably arise. It must likewise be borne in mind that the scribe is herself *totally ignorant* in regard to every hypothesis herein sought to be established, she never having received any previous instruction on such matters. The rebirth of the soul is now treated of, but only so to a certain extent. It is not to be supposed that the subject is herein *fully* unfolded, it is only glanced at; sufficient is, however, divulged to engender new and truer ideas than have hitherto gained admittance into any human mind.

Man is free to turn either to the right hand or to the left. He may go on and on in an evil course, if he so wills, till he dies as to the body. He is then active upon a new plane, and it is so similar to the one he has left, that he is not aware of any change having taken place. His body presents the same outward semblance, and his mental faculties are not, to appearance, in any way different to what they were when in the world: but his external memory is closed, so he remembers nothing whatever connected with his former life. The evil spirit is as free to work evil in the interiors of nature as he was in the exteriors; but the objects on which he can now alone exercise his propensities are as spiritual as himself. But his evil course having once been stayed by physical death, it will again be intercepted by spiritual death. Dissolution will occur in the interior, as it formerly did in the exterior regions of life.

The term of existence allotted to evil spirits is as various as that to which man is subject. But so soon as the "second death" has taken place, the spirit is with its God; it has then passed the boundary of all physical conditions; it has laid down its natural life, *interior* as well as exterior. It has traversed nature, but found therein no helpmeet; it was alone. It was not good for man to dwell alone; but wherefore did

God not provide this desolate one with a counterpart, even as He had done for His other sons? This question trenches on the foreknowledge of Deity. God is free to do as He will; He is the author of life, having life in Himself. It is the prerogative of Deity, and it is His will that man should possess it everlastingly: he can only do so by approximation to the Divine life. Evil is death, good is life; man may therefore exercise full freedom of choice in the matter of leading an evil life, but if he had control over life itself, he would never choose to die, either naturally or spiritually. Thus it will be seen that in the process of restoration to primeval conditions, no more restriction of the human will is exercised than applies to the duration of life; and the truth is, that a co-operation of man's will with the will of God is herein apparent, for all desire life, not death.

The intellectual or masculine nature is, in women, very nearly absorbed into their will or feminine nature, and hence they demonstrate intellectuality sometimes even in preponderance; but still the ultimation of it is in the person of man. On the other hand, men are sometimes more affectional than intellectual, nevertheless, that principle must be ultimated in the person of woman; if it be not so in each case, the manifestation of evil is inevitable.

The germ of a world is in the mind of God. He foreknows the course of every single particle of which it is composed. He knows what will be the life-experience of every individual spirit ere it leaves His presence. He provides for every contingency; not only does God do so with reference to the natural life of every human being, but He is omniscient over the immortal life. He provides for that ere the germ sets forth on its earthly pilgrimage. Thus the foreknowledge of God is a continual survey of humanity. He is not turned aside from His divine purpose by the will of man; for He knows the will of every creature ere it is formed into human shape. This is the view in which we must contemplate Deity. He is infinite; but the comprehensive bearing of that term is not sufficiently recognized: it means that God knows that which man can have no conception of; that which he has not yet the power to receive into his spirit; that which generation after generation will still be unable to fathom :—that is God.

Be not impatient with spirit-speech,—that it reveal not more than it does: human weakness must not be disregarded. The Lord is sustaining you in weakness, not in strength. He can make and He can unmake, but He considereth the nature of man : out of weakness shall come forth strength: and every riddle shall be expounded : but not till the hearing is more perfectly developed than it is at present. When I have advanced still further in this work, will a step have been gained, by means of which another, and yet another, may be attained; and at last we shall find that we have arrived at a temple not built with any human hand.

Before division of sex was effected, no sin was in existence; whether we take our standpoint of observation upon the earth or upon any orb rolling in space, the testimony will be the same—no babe born into the world is a whole or perfect Adam: but was so ere its descent into the natural ovary. The feminine portion of his being may be first ultimated, or it may be the masculine constituents: in either case, the spirit counterpart is in close interior consociation with the natural ultimation, and a communication of mental attributes is ever taking place between them; for the life of the one is in that of the other. This interior union is productive of results that are not, at present, comprehensible to the finite understanding. The spirit of the unborn partner is deriving momentary life and mental sustenance from the partner in nature, who is likewise dependent for every progressive development on the immaterialized spirit-partner. This is the course of all mundane ultimation: it is ever dependent upon spirit; and without an interior connection therewith can no physical life be sustained. It is not more essential to the full grown man or woman than to the babe of an hour.

No germ-soul comes forth of God in a divided state: every human monad must leave His person a perfect image and likeness of Himself: consequently, it can return so into the God-sphere from whence it emanated. The good man, the sainted martyr, is not perfect in the sight of God, neither are angels pure in His eyes; but He has formed every germ of human life with the capacity for final perfection, and this is the purpose of their birth into nature. Primitive conditions of life were "very good;" but now "there is no man good, no not one." Can the design of God in the creation of man be frustrated by the perverse will of man? Who says that it can, save that perverted will itself when allied to a false understanding of its own capabilities, ignorance of which is the source of all the error that mystifies humanity? I will shew that God's ways are equal: He does not create one for honor and another for dishonor: but they shall one and all be vessels of honor in His kingdom above. In nature, one is good, another is evil: one is comely, another deformed: but the natural appearance is not an admissible indication of the spiritual quality. The natural inclination of a good man leads him to a righteous course; the natural inclination of an evil man leads him to a depraved exhibition of life. But where is the responsibility? It resides in the *interiors* of the life: if depravity is there, then must malformation have been the cause of disorder. But man did not create himself, how then is he to be considered a responsible agent in the matter of good or evil choosing? If the will cannot be restrained from the commission of evil, then no natural ultimation of it is allowed, and the man so circumstanced will run an evil course, because he has no restraint in nature. That a man under such conditions can in nowise restrain his hand from the committal of evil deeds, is the providence of God; for if he could do so and did not, he would have no hold on eternal life, but must needs perish.

All human entities that are capable of salvation, without being subjected to the *second death*, are dual in the matter of natural ultimation; that is, every man has his feminine counterpart in the person of woman; and every woman has her masculine counterpart in the person of man. It is not necessary that the period of natural existence should be the same, or that the partners should come together, or even meet in nature; for they are spiritually united whether they do so or not: one partner may leave the world during the period of infancy, while the other partner may become well stricken in years: results are the same, though states will vary accordingly. Incongruous connections and uncongenial associations may take place in nature with the good as well as with the evil, but the spiritual condition is not interfered with. If counterparts, male and female, have received natural birth, the exhibition of life will be good; though with casual exceptions, no mortal being perfect; but, if either of the counterparts has been withheld from birth into nature, the exhibition of an evil life is inevitable; but the responsibility rests with the Creator, who has interposed the restraint so essential to everlasting life.

The *interior* natural life of the good is Adamic, that is, in undivided unity of sex; but the *interior* natural life of the wicked is in division. Dual unity does only exist in *interior* nature to which the evil man has no admittance; consequently he is an *external* natural being; he has no life more interior than the mere earth life, wherein he is not in the image and likeness of his Creator. But I have said that even the wicked are in the image and likeness of God in the *interiors* of their spirits. The soul-germ is so—it left the sanctuary of Deity whole and entire; but descended into the body only of woman and rested not in her spirit; but it has no counterpart in its own spirit, for it had left that in the germ-soul of its primitive God-like existence. Is it, therefore, unfairly dealt with at the hands of its Divine Parent? Nay, it is thus saved from the consequences of the curse, for if there be no will to good there is none to evil, the manifestation of which is the result of nature being under the curse of sin. Thus man is no more responsible for his disorderly acts than is the wild animal, for one is under the same influence as the other. That great intellectual endowments should sometimes be exhibited by evilly-disposed persons, is not surprising when we consider that all are *interiorly* Adam-man, and that he has no power to change one hair of his head.

The awakening of the spirit from the death of the body, will not release a man from his evil tendencies; he will rush into their indulgence just the same as he did in the world, and he will find the same field of opportunity open to him; for he is on the same plane of life as before he quitted the mortal state. The natural plane of life is divided into exterior and interior, or outward and inward conditions, or states of that same life. On the inward plane of life the wicked man is as wicked as on the outward; he is an evil spirit as well as an evil man. He is free to act as he will; he turneth to his former haunts, to the exercise of his disorderly practices. But he now reeleth not from the effects of natural narcotic; he stealeth not the gold of earth; he sweareth not in natural language; he has left all that with the body of clay. He is now a spirit, yet not in the image and likeness of his Creator; he is in an imperfect condition of human life. His tastes are natural only; and in every natural substance resides a spirit —a germ. Nothing that mortals view around them could otherwise minister to their immortal spirits. This is the secret of the dependence of matter upon spirit. There is a spirit—an interior essence in everything the earth contains, otherwise it could not contribute to the necessities of the soul as well as to those of the body of man.

The whole of man's system, physical as well as mental, is ever under the entire supervision of God; consequently he cannot turn either to the right hand or to the left, independently of permission and power delegated to him from God. This is the case with spirits as well as with men; and if they are evil, it is the will of God that they should be saved from the consequences of that evil which is death. Death is invariably the gate of life; therefore the wicked are led up to life through that gate. Death is life to the good man, and it is also life to the wicked man; but he—the wicked man—has no counterpart, no helpmeet, he must die the death of the soul; that is *his* gate of life. He must be born again in order to be relieved from the mark of Cain which is upon the brow of every murderer of innocence.

The death of the spirit is a natural as well as a spiritual death, it dies as die the men and the women of natural belongings. It is not difficult to see that it needs must be so, for the death of the body is but change of consciousness. If we could retain our spiritual consciousness whilst in that body, we should be external spiritual beings, as well as natural beings; it is consciousness that produces a world around us; if we become unconscious we cannot be said to live till its return restores us to our former position. In the case of the evil man, the natural mind which had attained to adult conditions in the life of the body, is dead; the spiritual mind which had also attained to adult conditions is likewise dead; and the germ-soul alone remains a living entity.

We now turn to the consideration of the means by which final restitution is to be effected. Man is in woman, and woman is in man; they are *interiorly* but one being. Inward spirit-union will produce offspring. What is the nature of these offspring—these children spiritually born in a region too remote for mortal perception? These come forth on a different plane of life to that on which the earthly parents are leading a conscious existence. The social economy of life is fraught with so much disorder that it is not possible for returning Adams to be again born into the world; but on that interior plane we term *interior nature* they are a mighty host, "men of renown that were of old," born unto women by virtue of *interior* marriage ties, consummated within the recesses of the spirit. It is in *nature* that these sons have re-birth, yet nature bears no witness to the fact. It is not possible for it to do so since *interior* perception has been closed to mortals. They are now oblivious to the inner life of the spirit; they are benumbed by the frosts and the snows of earth; their fine sensitive spirit-organs are inert, and even comprehension faileth.

The division of sex which took place in the garden of God, is the divine utterance in nature,—Let all men come unto me that I may save them. Let no man say he cannot come on account of natural hindrance: "Go out into the highways, and search the byeways, and compel them to come in unto me." The coercion hereby implied is not referable to the natural mind, that is free to work out its own destruction if it be so inclined. The will of the spirit is free to work out its own death; but after that cometh resurrection and life. It might as well be imagined that a spirit could make himself God, as that he can change the decrees of Omnipotence. All are created "very good," but if they choose to work iniquity in the wilderness of nature, they can do so, for they are there as free as God Himself who has made them to be so.

The infringement of the law of order having taken place in nature, it is *there* that reparation must be made. The immortal can never again become mortal; yet he can be born again, not after the flesh mortally, but after the spirit spiritually. Man cannot again enter into his mother's womb and be born into the world, but he can enter into such *interior* relations with woman as to be born of her into primitive conditions of spiritual life. The only condition upon which man can inherit eternal life being birth from woman; it is not more essential that he should be born of her into natural than into spiritual life, for one is wholly dependent upon the other.

It has been shewn that the spirit is born of God. If woman give it natural birth it is a babe in the world; but if she give it spirit-birth only, then is she the mother of an Adam, for he was undivided ere the curse was pronounced upon the birth of nature. That spirit-son will be a man-Adam, not a child; childhood being a state consequent upon the declension. These statements are here merely reverted to as necessary to be borne in mind, in order to the promotion of understanding in regard to that which is to be still further revealed. Birth from woman was essential to the advent of the Lord Christ in nature; and that was essential to the redemption of the human race. Hence it may be inferred that it is equally essential to the maintenance of the purpose which that redemption has effected. If it were not possible for the Messiah to come without the aid of woman, how should it be possible for mankind to be released from flesh-bondage independent of her co-operation? The thread of life is one; it is also a ladder by means of which the angels descend as well as ascend.

The life of woman is not fully developed till the days of her childhood are past. Then commences a physical condition which had in her no previous existence. This womanly development is identical with her restoration to primitive states of inward life. She has then become "woman;" she has conceived seed; she can henceforth bear children unto the Lord; she can "be fruitful and multiply." Herein we find that the Lord hath not spoken in vain. The seed of the woman hath bruised the serpent's head. The seed of man hath likewise done so; for, as shewn above, there is no woman independent of man, neither is man independent of woman. Previous to their *interior* union of spirit, can no manifestation of womanhood or of manhood take place; but so soon as that can be consummated, so soon can spirit-offspring be produced. Nature does not exhibit any outward effect that is not consequent upon interior causes, but what those causes are, no man may tell. The cause of that change of physical arrangement, which becomes apparent in both sexes at the period of adolescence, is herein divulged. They are born into the world men and women, that they may replenish the earth, and have dominion over it. In the recesses of every human spirit goes on a work connected with the universe. The man who has found no helpmeet in the world, does so in the spirit; and likewise the lone woman, she is invariably united to her soul's partner, and together they form but one being, in that sphere which I must designate *interior nature*. The manifestation of spirit-birth takes place at periodically recurring seasons; the affinity of these states with natural childbirth is apparent.

The subject must be taken up at the various points of observation, and allowance must be made for the limited means attainable for its complete elucidation. The man of sin is *interiorly* an Adam just as much so as the man of exalted virtue, but he has not entered upon natural life under the same conditions; no helpmeet has been provided for him; he has no counterpart; she has not descended with him into natural ultimation: if he had a helpmeet in nature as well as in spirit, he could be regenerated upon the same plane as that on which the good man makes manifest his good inherent qualities. But the undisguised sinner is not a responsible agent: the sexual division having failed to place him in the condition pertaining unto the saint. Herein we view the providence of God for the restoration of the whole human race to their primeval unity in Himself. I must, however, demand patience, for this theme is of vast extent. I am in my sphere, and the scribe is in hers, yet without a conjunction of ability no outward effect can take place; and the spring of action has to be arranged as we proceed from one point to another, consequently, the course of this treatise will be irregular, yet we shall be enabled to go forward with entire confidence in the power that is directing us both to the same end. The veil is, however, but very partially removed from before her eyes, and she is ignorant of that to which I must now draw attention. Human beings are their own guardians, they have been in celestial states of life, as previous to the severance of Adam and Eve. That state remains an ever present one within. It influences every succeeding stage of life,—every subsequent expericnce through which that same spirit has to pass. It is thus that mankind are their own guardians, and their own ministering spirits. None other can be, no amount of sympathetic affection will enable one individual spirit to participate in the experience of another.

Had man never declined into perverted states the spirit-birth from woman had not been needed. The birth from Adam proper would have at once ushered him into life, and there would have been no division of sex possible; but as this supervened, the birth from woman became a necessity. The first birth, that of nature into spiritual capabilities; the second, into spirit with celestial capabilities. It is not at present possible to elaborate this vast theme; but it is only necessary to draw an outline to be filled in at some future period. The birth of man into celestial conditions cannot yet be treated of, as the scribe is unprepared to sustain the conceptions to which it would give rise.

The severance of Eve from man is, at the same time, a severance of woman from woman. It is the outbirth of natural womanhood from the inward feminine principle of man's life. But, lest contradiction be supposed to exist between this statement and those which have preceded it, I shall still further explain. This feminine principle, this Eve which remained in Adam, was not cursed, for she had never been drawn forth into outward life. The woman who stood at Adam's side was alone the inheritor of that curse. That is the woman now in nature, she is cursed in her separation from Adam. The life of both must perish if they be not *inwardly* united, and if only so in nature and not so in the spirit, they will die the death of the soul. The case with every evil man is this, he is an Adam only in the flesh of nature; but the good man is an Adam in the spirit as well, and the germ-soul is therefore in the woman not in the spirit, but in the natural life of his feminine counterpart, who is the Eve taken out of his perfect life in God. This is the case with the good; they have only given of their natural life to the female counterpart, consequently she is a natural woman, but inwardly she is in the man's primeval life. She is his germ-soul. But if the case be reversed, and the man be in evil conditions, the germ-soul will be retained within his terrestrial life, and the woman, his counterpart, will be unultimated, for she will be in him still, and there will be no birth for her: he has not obeyed the command "be fruitful, multiply, and replenish the earth, and have dominion over it;" false seed will be engendered, adulterous union will take place, for there is no wife.

The Lord was in that condition in which man must needs be evil; but He being God overcame that which man could not, and His Eve principle being wholly within and not any portion thereof without Him, He united the condition of man in the good state and man in the evil state with woman in exterior as well as interior relation to Him. This is the meaning of His being both masculine and feminine. The Lord was so in externals as well as in internals; but not until He had vanquished death and the grave. *Then* was He man and woman in one substance and form, and so different was He then in outward appearance, that He was not known either of Mary or His disciples : thus shewing the change He had effected even in the natural formation of man. The Lord was a natural man, a spiritual man, and a divine man. In nature He had no counterpart, in the spirit He had none, in His divine essence He had a Divine Counterpart, but without any ultimation. In this respect He was in the position of the evil man. He, the Lord, met him upon his own ground, or plane of life; in every degree of that life conditions are equal. The good man is differently constituted altogether; he has a counterpart in nature and in spirit. It matters not whether their union be consummated in the world or not; in the present order of society it is very generally reserved till the mortal has passed into another stage of being, and it will save him from the second death which occurs to the evil.

The case must now be shewn with reference to woman. She has no life independent of man, for she is a dependent creation, not directly but indirectly emanating from God. She is, however, a direct emanation from God in so far as the germ-soul is concerned; that is, whether we say God created man or whether we should say God created woman, it is the same thing, if we do not refer to the woman *separated* from Adam; but as God did not live on earth as woman, we may be sure there is no germ of human life contained in the person of woman, it is whole and entire in man; thus it is that male children are more esteemed throughout the entirety of humanity; for the principle of feminine subjection is from this root; and although in civilized nations the case is somewhat reversed, still nature will assert the fact. Woman is a purely natural being; her existence is in that of man; and when she becomes a spirit, she is ever anxious to return into the bosom of her husband, not to retain any separate identity from his; for she knows she cannot do so and live; neither could he unless the natural stay of his life be restored; for every degree of human life must have a natural foundation.

The one who now turns away her ear from this announcement will perhaps be the first to seek its fulfilment; so hard is it for nature to comprehend spirit, and for natural feeling to yield obedience to the demands of Deity; but dwell upon the conception, ye wives of men, and it will produce in your souls the paradise you otherwise vainly anticipate. Blessed is she who can receive this saying. The one of slow comprehension is not dull in the spirit; therefore the truth is now made known, and if any *female form* can be glorified into an angel of light, then will *man* sink down to the level of the brutes that perish; for they are male and female, never one in and with the other; this is the difference between man and brute; the one has woman within him, the other has the female without him.

We now turn to the contemplation of Deity in the perfect form of man with woman in His life, not outwardly manifest, but inwardly existing. The Lord returned from Hades, bearing His divine feminine principle into natural life; it so overspread His mien and visage, that He could be no longer recognized as Jesus Christ. He was then God in all fulness; He was then the natural God; He was divine and natural; He had put on woman, and woman was now in the image and likeness of God, man and woman were made one in nature,—in spirit, as they had ever been in their divine relation to Deity. Mary did not know her Lord. She turned, and supposed she saw but "the gardener." Verily, she,—woman,—is still in the garden. She is born for higher things, and her eyes are made for beholding a more glorious vision. Mary will know the Lord, but not till He shall call her. He that is born of the spirit, is spirit; and he that is born of the flesh, is flesh. Give no heed to the man of flesh, for he can only teach of such things as pertain unto the flesh; but spirit teacheth of spirit, and spiritual things must be spiritually discerned. The Lord is man, woman in the spirit of woman, and woman in the nature of woman. He is also woman in her ability to produce offspring and to rear up sons, for to her belong peculiar characteristics in which man has no part. She is a mother in Israel, not only so as respects her body, but as respects that spirit of nature by which she holds her life. She can bestow upon her sons such qualities of heart and mind as do not pertain unto the natural development of man; and thus she contributes to that position in the universe which I designate Adamic, the natural qualifications for which reside wholly with woman. In this view we see the Lord as a divine natural Woman as well as Man; consequently nature would not long contain Him; it buoyed Him upon its pinions, and He could no more be seen of men; but like as they have seen Him go, so shall they see Him come again with power and great glory. That is, when their sight again becomes divine enough to behold divine objects; when nature, spirit, and divinity culminate in one point.

The passage of Scripture in which mention is made of "men of renown, mighty men that were of old," is the least understood of any the Bible contains. But exposition of it shall now be made. The mention of these heroes has remained a dead letter to all. Some have misrepresented it, none have understood it. It is not for any work the human hand is set on, to claim the prerogative of infallible truth; but so long as this pen can trace my words, so long shall truth of a higher order than has yet received natural ultimation, descend to earth. But wherefore now, and not at any previous age, are such mysteries revealed to mortals? They are not aware that close, very close within the veil of mortal flesh, goes on the work of final restitution to lost primeval conditions of life. Spirits are busy with spirits; mortals with mortals. Nurse your infants; educate them up to man's estate; but know! that for every babe a mother gives birth to, birth is given seventy times seven in the spirit-womb within the natural ovary. Know! that mortal flesh is, in a sense, immortal; that the passing month gives notice of the ascent of a soul-germ on its way back to paradise and God. Believe it not if you cannot see that it needs must be so; be not hard of hearing. I am not able to certify the fact, but I propound it as a fact, that no one can gainsay. The germ of a resuscitated devil is ever gestating in the womb of woman. And it is born into the spiritual region called Eden, or interior nature: then is the natural body removed; it passes away, and woman may henceforth know that she has been the medium for the restoration to primeval life of a "lost soul." She then receives another implantation of returning human seed; it germinates; comes to maturity in her person; and the like results ensue. This is the case with every woman, whether she be in the position of a wife or not; and that it does occur indiscriminately, be she well disposed or ill disposed, is a certain indication that, *inwardly*, every woman in existence is standing upon the same platform, and is under the same universal law of God's own appointment for the salvation of the human race. That I assume too much in this hypothesis is not likely, when we consider the physical conditions essential to preservation of health in woman. It is not however an arrangement exclusively applicable to the human subject; but is found to exist in all female animals; exemplifying in their prolification the perfect law of representation from which they exist, and by which their life is sustained. These things are of weighty import. This knowledge is not merely speculative, it is of vital utility, and ever was so; but, owing to human depravity, it could not find access into any human mind. Such things do not come within the scope of mortal comprehension unassisted by spiritual revealment.

———

The spirit of God moveth upon the waters of strife, but confusion ceaseth not. Death is sent forth on its mission of love to mankind. Its *second* arrow pierceth the soul of the wicked; they die, and there is then no more life in the soul than in the body, the whole man is extinct in so far as nature is concerned; but being *interiorly* in the form of God, no death can touch that interior essence which has constituted him man. That germ is then returned to God without possessing any concomitant of nature; for it did not attract to itself any particle thereof either terrestrial or spiritual. Thus it is that God provides for the restoration of "lost souls;" they are cared for ere they set forth on the pilgrimage through nature. They are destined for holy uses. Without their aid all must perish, with their aid all men live; they purge the land, they purify the water of life. These evil beings are the scavengers of humanity; and in the performance of their work, effect their own salvation. Thus the spark flies up to Him who has enkindled it, and lost humanity is saved. The man of sin is bearing in his person the curse pronounced upon Adam in the garden of Eden. If it were possible for one of these to become an angel, without undergoing the *second death,* heaven would not stand, for one of its pillars would be removed; but as it is, the foundation is eternally established, and cannot be removed.

This is the position I assume for the wicked, be they in male or female forms. They take the disease, that we may not be infected by it; they are therefore our finite Redeemers: Christ is our infinite—our God Redeemer. They are bearing our sins, and are suffering for our infirmities in the *natural* degree; Christ did so in the *spiritual* degree. The malaria of spirit has been absorbed into the person of Jesus; the malaria of nature is absorbing into the persons of evil men and women, who are very sick with *our* infirmities, and are ever dying of *our* maladies. They die the death of the soul; they then live the life of the germ-soul; it is pure, untouched by the breath of nature; it is infantile, innocent, irresponsible, a child of God, one who has never left His presence. It is then to be incarnated in the *inner sanctuary* of natural gestation.

The soul is ever renewing its vital energies in God; but it is likewise ever parting with these energies: they are evolving upon lower and lower planes of life, till finally they become purely natural; and that which was originally received fresh from the eternal fount of life, is naturalized into the corporeal frame of man. This is the course of all life; it is the breath of God, divine in its primary degree, spiritual in its second, and natural in its third and last degree. But it is also compound in its division into those various degrees of reception by the human subject. It is interior and exterior divine; interior and exterior spiritual; interior and exterior natural: this last degree of reception ultimates and includes the whole in the natural mind and body of man, who is not more dependent upon God in one sphere of life than in another. The Lord is thus the perpetual sustainer of the body as well as of the spirit, and of the soul-germ; His action is simultaneous upon each and every sphere and phase of human existence. Therefore, every bodily effect, no matter what it may be, is the exponent of some spiritual effect; and that again is dependent upon some still more interior effect, which God is producing upon the germ of life that is ever in His immediate presence. In this way we are born again from God moment by moment. This is the rebirth of humanity, effected by our Almighty Parent in the supreme degree of His action upon us. But, we are in nature dependent upon one another; we must, therefore, place ourselves in that relation to each other that God has Himself appointed for the furtherance of His beneficent designs towards us.

We have seen that the physical frame is adapted to carry out the highest purposes of God; that it is ever doing His work of redemption; and that it cannot be sustained in life under any other condition. But we find there is a period when the ability to give birth in nature altogether ceases. Women in whom the childbearing season has closed, are exercising the function of maternity upon a higher plane of existence than was previously open to their ministration; they are doing so upon the celestial plane of life, in which the flesh covering, which I have said passes away, is not needed. These are the Sarahs and the Elizabeths of the race, who can still bring forth sons independent of natural law; as Isaac, and John the Baptist. The birth of these sons was natural, but not outwardly so; they moved through life in a sphere as distinct from that of outward natural life, as does the spirit after passing from the earth life. But in order to substantiate such a statement as this I must be allowed time; for, though in my present sphere time has no existence, the scribe is not independent thereof. Woman can give birth to offspring that need not even the interior co-operation of nature; but these are whole Adams—undivided human beings; they are spirits who have returned to the estate of primeval Adam without the passage through spiritual death. The good are thus born again. They are gestated in the spirit of woman so deeply, so interiorly, that nature makes no report, takes no part in the transaction. Woman has then become the mother of returning Adams, not into spirit-life, not into Eden, but into that paradise which is nearest to the throne of God,—into that primitive residence of man in which he was originally born of God as Adam-man. This thing is complicated to the natural understanding. The woman who has arrived at that period of life wherein no natural seed can be any more conceived of her, is yet able to give re-birth to the righteous; no longer so to the unrighteous. The good have to be born again as well as the evil. The good must be reborn into celestial conditions, the bad into spiritual conditions, and both must finally regain paradise by birth from interior womanhood. This process is ever going on. The power to give that inward celestial rebirth is not, however, received by woman till the days of her youth are past, then has she returned to celestial capabilities, and she can henceforth be the mother of celestial, as she formerly was of spiritual Adams.

This revelation may be still further elucidated as we advance in the present course; but at this point we must turn aside to complete the description of the fate of the "lost," for there is an interval between the death of the body and that of the soul. Death is the gate of life to all as at present constituted. The good man dies in the body, the evil man does so in the spirit as well; but after that he is born to die no more; he has reached the same plane as that on which the good sustain life. Their transition from state to state is not painful; to the wicked it is: they die; but the good are caused to fall into a "deep sleep" or trance, from which they are reborn. It is a painful disease of which the wicked spirit dies, occasioned by the indulgence of evil habits. He is not confined in any hell that he would fain escape from—he is in perfect freedom, and may roam whither he pleases, only, he may not infest the good, nor injure his fellows; he may associate with whom he will, but must be governed by the law of the spirit land, and it is as imperative and as legitimate in its demand upon him, as was the case in the sphere he has left. In this interior region, the wicked man is as wicked as he was on earth. But there are degrees of evil: the manifestation varies in every individual, some being only slightly divergent from the right course, others more so, and others again are an abomination to humanity. These will, one and all, find their true level; they will not suffer more than their natural proclivities entail upon them; but they are now fatal to the soul. The body may suffer torture even when the spirit is in a good condition; disease is experienced by the most virtuous characters; mental suffering is also endured by the saint, the consequence of evil tendencies inherent in every mortal. Wherever there is evil, whether in the natural or in the spiritual world, there is hell. The length of time, to use earth's language, during which the hell of wicked spirits may endure is ever dependent upon individual states. If the spirit is only partially infected with the plague, he will remain an inhabitant of interior nature till his disease has infected his whole spiritual life, which then becomes as extinct as his natural life. There is then no more of him, his germ-soul has to be reborn of woman into that sphere which is just within the mortal flesh.

The Lord has prevision; He knows that a human spirit has left his sanctuary who will not continue in the straight and narrow way of righteousness: He provides for that spirit, that it may return unto Him, leaving its defiled nature in nature. For this holy purpose the counterpart is retained—natural life is not allowed it. If it be a female that is to be born into the world under this condition, then the masculine principle is withheld from the restrictions of flesh bondage. No severance has occurred in the garden of Eden, or the interiors of natural life. The whole cause of disorder lies at this root. The man or the woman so born into earth-life is inevitably wicked, and consequently dies the second death—that of the spirit. But God is not angry with it; He has *purposely* made that provision against everlasting disorder.

junction with the natural counterpart in the body of nature; and when the evil man or evil woman is dead as to that body, the manifestation of evil still goes on in the *interiors* of natural life, because that is the inevitable consequence of the non-severance of masculine and feminine principles. That the manifestation of an evil life should invariably result from a disproportionate intercourse of masculine with feminine nature, is not apprehensible to the merely natural mind; but, when it is remembered that the whole economy of life is entirely dependent upon sexual division, we can understand that any infringement of, or interference with, that rule, must occasion very stupendous consequences to the soul of man.

These doctrines have never heretofore been preached in any human ear; therefore a vast amount of accommodation to the natural capacity is requisite, and must be admitted; very faint is the impress that can yet be made by them upon any mind, however elevated, or accustomed to the contemplation of spiritual themes. Hence much allowance must be granted on account of the extreme intricacy of the subject; but, it is very possible to attain unto a just conception of it, to a certain extent, and that is all that can, in the present state of human development, be expected. The counterpart is, by the Divine will, reserved from natural ultimation; consequently, the evilly disposed man, or woman, will expire *in the spirit* as well as in the body, and then cometh life and righteousness. This is the will and the mandate of Omnipotence.

This is the sum of the remarks on reserved human counterparts. Nature is the plane of all evil demonstration. When the soul is released from *inner* or spirit nature, there is then no room for such disorderly experience: the soul returns to God who gave it, and who thus makes provision for the return of every soul unto Himself,—into His own life,— His own paradise, wherein all men and all things are "very good."

But, before this final restoration can be effected, the soul must die as to its perverted will; it is not free from the bonds of corruption; it haunts the former corporeal frame left in the world; it infests the loathsome grave; the worm and maggot become its companions; it is with dead men's bones, and all uncleanness. There is weeping and gnashing of teeth,—there is groaning, shrieking, and bitter lamentation. But, the death of the wicked does not consist in the experience of these woes to all eternity. The spirit is now distressed; it descries the sorrows that belong unto evil; it prays for release,—the wicked spirit prays,—the hardened soul weeps,— the proud supplicate,—the wolf becomes the lamb. The Shepherd of Israel finds it,—carries it in His bosom,—bears it up to His own sanctuary. "It is finished." The work He came into nature to accomplish is performed in that soul; hell and destruction are vanquished, the spirit is at rest with its

God; from thence it will come again whole and entire; it will receive re-birth. It has been stated how that is; but let it not be supposed that the death of the wicked ushers them at once into the kingdom of everlasting peace.

The natural life of evil does not admit of any torture or suffering of any kind; it would not advance regeneration, but would, on the contrary, tend to retard it; but, so soon as all natural concomitant is put off, so soon does hell torment become a conscious experience, the sole purpose of which is to promote aversion to evil habits, contrition, and desire to abandon every kind of spiritual wickedness. This is the inevitable result; in every instance the consequences are identical: every sheep of the Lord's flock is thus, by their *own desire*, rescued from the flame that is not quenched—where the worm dieth not, and where there is wailing and gnashing of teeth. These things are of painful contemplation, therefore we desire not to prolong the subject. The extent of experience differs in every case.

The doctrine herein propounded in respect of evil emancipation, is not so fully elucidated as it may be at a future period; but it is, in its present form, quite indispensable to the substantiation of the truth of universal restitution to the God-like image into which *all* and *every* man is born. Without death can no man see life; nature must die. With the righteous death is a calm sleep; like the martyr Stephen, they fall "asleep," they cannot be said to die; they put off nature in a "deep sleep;" they are then with their God who needeth not to seek them, for they are in His house, having never left it.

The re-birth of the spirit is identical with the restoration to primeval unity of masculine and feminine attributes, which is essential to the inheritance of eternal life; on no other condition can death be excluded, its occurrence being the consequence of sexual division.

The Lord is with the evil in death as in life; He is their staff and their stay; but in unconsciousness. The well disposed receive the Lord, consciously seeking Him; the evilly disposed seek Him not, but receive Him unconsciously. The life of evil is absorbed into the person of Jesus. He takes the malady,—dies of it on the cross,—destroys it in Himself,—overcomes evil with good,—conquers death and the grave. The Lord Jesus does this for every human being. A wicked man has no care for the things that belong unto life and righteousness; he hungereth only after such things as belong unto death; he seeks death, not life: good only is life.

The life of man is immortal only by reason of its approximation to the Divine Author of life. Man has lost the God-image into which he was created; the drawing forth of woman into nature has deprived him of it; she is not in the image of God any more than is man; but *within* she retains it, though unknown to herself, and must needs act in accordance with her inward formation. She can, as we have shewn, send forth *spirit-born* sons in the likeness of their father Adam; and she can in no way stay the operation of her mission in nature. Thus she, by whom the God-image was taken away from the person of man, restores it whole and unblemished.

Woman is strong unto salvation. "Whatsoever openeth the womb is mine," (Exod. xiii. 2.) "The fruit of the womb is His reward," (Psalm cxxvii. 3.) This is the language of inspiration; it is the voice of Deity making itself to be heard in the council chambers of humanity; it is the fruit of the womb that is so important to God that it can become a recompence unto Him! Can man give back any good thing to God? He can but give again that he has received from God,—he can give back nothing save his own soul. It was the Lord's ere it came into conscious existence. It lived in Deity ere it lived in nature; and, now that it has been born of woman into that nature, it shall be *re-born* of her into her *primitive* nature which is in the breast of man.

In this estate come forth the sons of God. "Mighty men" are they; "men of renown, which were of old;" princes in the camp of the Lord, with power over the beasts of the earth (2 Sam. xxiii. 20); dauntless in danger. These are the men who "possess the gates of their enemies,"—these be they who were once "lost sheep." They have gone up to the source of strength, and have come again from the storehouse of Deity laden with His might; and they have brought back their craven nature made valiant by

His greatness—empowered by His might. They are the children who "speak with the enemy in the gate," (Psalm cxxvii.,) that opens into the fallen condition from which they have been redeemed; and they can pass scatheless through the camp of their enemies to fetch water from the well of Bethlehem (1 Chron. xi. 17, 18). They are *ever* fetching water from the spring at Bethlehem; but it is poured out upon the earth, unappropriated by the natural mind. When the Lord is followed to the cross, we forget that He is preparing to rise into everlasting glory. When we see that the water of life is the blood of man, we refuse to drink it; but if we knew that it is the blood, or might, of God, we should long for it as did David when he said, "Oh! that one would bring me water from the well of Bethlehem!" The Scriptures are not what they seem; they are *very much more* than they appear to be. Nature has never yet been sounded to her lowest depths; and her highest capacity of sustaining human life has never been revealed as at this hour; for the king is languishing for need of the water of Bethlehem.

It is for none to scan the present phase of spiritual revealment; it comes, none know how; it is given, none know why; it is brought to pass in the present day of the world, and was not at any past epoch, and is not deferred to any future age. None can tell the reason for this; but that there is a reason none may doubt. The moment that one dispensation expires another is born; and no instant of time is void of its appropriate dispensation. The day of our Lord's gospel advent had many good things in store for men, but they could not then be shewn forth. There are everlasting store houses in the breast of God, and He breathes forth their treasures into the lungs of humanity so soon as spiritual life can be thereby promoted.

In woman is life and resurrection: she has the seed of Christ within her, hence she is very honorable in His sight. For righteousness and for mercy's sake has He come forth of woman. She is in her true position only in the breast of man; but, for righteousness and for judgment, and for mercy's sake, is she brought forth out of that, her primitive sanctuary.

Now, it is felt by many good and loving wives that they would rather retain *external* severance with *internal* union only. This is a consequence of the prevalence of that disorder which is so extensively spread over the face of every land. The female who would rather retain her separate individuality, is not aware for what reason she was severed; she is not conscious of any hindrance to her individual salvation in that fact; and she is averse to the idea of entering upon a condition of life so entirely beyond the grasp of her imagination to conceive. In this we see how impossible it is for natural life to proceed in harmony with the decrees of God; for although without union no flesh can attain salvation, yet it is refused acceptance so soon as the true conditions on which it can alone be obtained become known. But life is involuntary, therefore woman cannot, by her inclination, either hinder or accelerate its progress to final consummation. She was not consulted in the matter of her first birth, neither is she in that of her second birth into the unity of righteousness; the one involves the other; if one had not been, neither could the other; if Adam had not required an external helpmeet, no woman would have been seen among the hosts that people the earth; but for righteousness and for purification she is drawn forth of man's frame; she was one with his spirit, but could not remain so.

Woman is spiritually prolific, whether she be chaste or unchaste. How can an unchaste woman be productive of chaste fruit? The harlot is usually unprolific of offspring. She has destroyed the capacity of containing life in her womb; but she has an interior or spiritual womb into which mortal seed cannot enter. That chamber is undefiled. Is there not something telling us, that the mass of pollution we behold was once a smiling infant, free from mortal taint? Ere the breath of man breathed upon her cheek, it was as fair within as it may now *appear* without. Where is that fair childish form? It has sunk to rest upon a mother's breast—that breast is God's. That breast pillows every head, whether it ache in nature or not, whether it be pure in nature or not. God has taken woman out of man, and has placed her in the world; shall He not be responsible for the consequences of that act? She has been much abused by her protector, man; she has borne his sins and carried his infirmities to her own shame, dishonor, and death. She has mourned over her children, giving them birth in mortal anguish. She has been subdued in her weakness, despised in her office, shunned in her degradation: man's helpmeet in time; in eternity his counterpart, —his *inmost* self. In her capacity, the helpmeet of Deity; for she is the means by which He is saving man. The day of the world is passing; it will soon be very far spent; then will woman be seen clothed with the splendours of the Sun of Righteousness. Human souls come forth of woman into every life of possible inheritance; they who go up to possess the land must all be born again of woman, even because she is one with Christ in a way that men are not. Men are born of God into man's estate; that is, equally masculine and feminine; but the Lord, by virtue of the feminine principle in Himself, made woman out of "the rib" taken from Adam. Hence she holds her life more exclusively in the *Humanity* of Deity than does man. She is flesh of his flesh, and bone of his bone. So is Christ. He comes forth of His own flesh; for, if He had no affinity with it, He could never have been born of it. No man contributed to the birth of Christ into nature;

F 3

but, Mary must be affianced to Joseph ere she can be accessible to the overshadowing power of the Highest, and receive the Lord Jesus into her womb.

A babe is not the offspring of one parent more than another, both are equal in the work; nature requires two principles to be combined ere she can produce a human being; Christ required not the *external* nature of man, but He did require his *interior* nature, otherwise He could not redeem it. He took it from Joseph, who is the type of the race, and He combined it with Mary's *internal* feminine principle. *Interiorly*, Mary and Joseph are one Adam, in nature divided for the divine purpose, in the accomplishment of which they are employed.

The Lord died as die the wicked spirits. *This* is the death endured by Christ; on this crucifix He suffered,—on this cross He hung,—on the Calvary that no mortal eye may scan. On that *spirit*-mount did Christ the Righteous redeem the murderer and thief, and every malefactor that ever drew, or may draw, breath in natural life. Christ died, not that the righteous might live: He saved them in Eden when He divided man from woman; that was the redemption of the righteous: it needed not His flesh advent: it was in the spirit they needed the physician, and He there and then ministered to, and provided for, the inner necessities of the spirit. Thus the righteous are *spiritually* redeemed by Him; the evil are *naturally* redeemed by Him. The Lord entered into spirit-life bearing with Him the flesh covering of His terrestrial manifestation, but it was not such flesh as that worn by mortals; it was the clothing of the spirit, inasmuch as it was formed of the spiritual essence of that outer flesh. But we will further explain elsewhere. The body of our Lord returned to the inner sanctuary whence it had, at birth, come forth, and there it united natural, with spiritual or interior natural substance. It bound up fibre by fibre, and restored the original formation of the body. It became the form of Adam previous to his deep sleep. The Lord did this in His own person, producing a corresponding effect upon every human being that had ever, or should ever, be born of Him. He is infinite; independent of all time; past, present, and to come, is all one before Him. He sees the universe as a unit. He acts;—and it is His providence for the moment and for the age, and for the coming cycle of ages. This is Jesus Christ, the Son of Man, and Son of God,—the God.

The whole plan of redemption is now complete. The framework of nature is infilled with the Spirit of divine life. The Lord Jesus Christ is the soul of every man, woman, and child in existence; every one is an interior Adam, and Christ has rescued him from eternal death. Death of the body still remains, and death of the spirit still remains: but, Adam is redeemed from the death of the germ-soul. Soul is a term applicable to every degree of human life, natural, spiritual, and celestial: therefore, we use the word *germ-soul* in preference to that of spirit germ, for, that is only applicable to the life of exterior, exclusive of interior nature, which must not be excluded from our thoughts when contemplating the final destiny of man. He is as dependent for life upon one kingdom as upon another; and whether his spirit be saved in one or in another, his whole being is participant. The soul-germ does not pertain to one kingdom of life more than to another, but is ever indrawn during the natural life of spirits as well as that of men. Nature is ever predicable of mankind so long as they retain sex conditions, which are nature's stronghold: when sex division is abolished, nature is vanquished, dies, and is no more a human experience.

But nature has a germ-soul within, as truly as the human life it has nourished and sustained. That germ-soul of nature is the body of Adam, not of Eve; she was not born in nature, but from the soul of Adam; consequently, woman has not the same hold on nature that man has. Woman is an after thought, a subsequent creation: she does not proceed direct from God as does man: she is only mediately related to the Divine Being: she has come of an interior blending of life with the life of man: he has himself given her birth though in unconsciousness and in entire dependence upon the divine Parent.

The Lord made woman <u>out of</u> man, not woman <u>with</u> man: but He did, in the first instance, make

Adam as man and woman in one person and form. That was not making woman; it was making a man that should be as much one as the other. If it had been said that the Lord God made woman, and that, in process of time she was put into "a deep sleep," in which the Lord took one of her ribs and made it into a man;—the case would have been in nowise altered. The first creation would have been just the same; no difference would have existed. The woman would have been commanded to be fruitful and multiply just as well and just as appropriately as the command was given to Adam; and it would have been obeyed in precisely the same manner in which it was obeyed; for conditions are equal. Now, that this was not the order in which creation was established, shews us that a difference of identity exists between the separated woman, or Eve, and the feminine principle identical with Adam as he first came into being from God. The Adamic woman is still identical with man, she never comes forth of him; but, the body of Adam has contributed to the formation of the Eve now at his side. She is therefore flesh of his flesh and bone of his bone: she is called "woman" by virtue of that, but in consequence of her severance, she is called "Eve." This distinction shall be still further explained; but, for the present, we bear upon the point of nature having no part in that feminine principle which is still and ever has been in man. The man Adam is not to be identified with woman as she appears in the world, but he is one with her germ-soul; and woman is not to be identified with man as he is seen in the world, but she is one with his germ-soul: there is but one germ-soul for each. The process of Eve-severance took place quite independent of the germ-soul: that was not in the least affected thereby: it did not come forth into external life at all: it remained in Adam: it was not drawn forth with Eve: therefore she has no eternal life out of, or distinct from, Adam. She is flesh of his flesh and bone of his bone; that is, her natural life is in, and with, his: one life, not two lives. Man is, therefore masculine and feminine in his interiors, but woman is only so in her exteriors; inwardly, she has no existence out of Adam, or man. This is the point to which particular attention must now be paid, for without it, no understanding of that which is to follow can be expected.

The "lost sheep" are they who have in nature no counterpart, be it male or female, as the case may be: but, for the present, we are treating of Adam, not of Eve, save as she is connected with him. A man is evilly disposed, in consequence of his feminine portion not being drawn forth into natural existence. He cannot live without a helpmeet, and he has none that can minister to him in the place of woman; his own affections are beasts of the field; they are wild beasts, and are devouring one another; they are his enemies instead of being his companions; they are successful in their malevolence towards him, for, at last, they destroy his life in nature altogether. These wild disorderly affections, lusts, and desires of the flesh are, nevertheless, dependent upon man for their existence; for he engenders them in himself, and gives them a name and a standing in nature; he gives them spirit-birth as properties existing in himself, and they give to him the means of restoration to his original status in the Divine mind; for, they devour his natural life, and send him back to God. These beasts—these evil affections, slay the wicked man. Jesus saved the good in Eden; but to the wicked He said, "Cursed art thou; upon thy belly shalt thou go, and dust shalt thou eat all the days of thy life." This sentence has not been literally fulfilled either in man or beast; but, in the spirit it is so, not as regards any beast of the field, but as regards the wily fiend within the human breast: this serpent does, to this day, go upon its belly, and does continue to eat dust. This animal propensity, typified by a serpent, is the unregenerate human heart; it is natural and spiritual, not divine in its origin, therefore not immortal: it grovelleth in nature alone,—this is indicated by the curse of going upon its belly; it cannot be elevated above the standard of corporeal life, and it there aggrandizes itself, and is even wiser than the children of light. But, the evil man is a resident in *interior* as well as in exterior nature; he is a serpent in both, and as the beast of the field, so he perishes. The germ-soul is, however, immortal.

The Lord is not magnified by the death of any human spirit; and as He does all things well, so He hath appointed all men once to die: after that cometh resurrection and life. The Lord is, then, magnified by the *second* death of the wicked: they pass from *that* death,—from evil,—unto life and righteousness. They are an heritage of the Lord; were an abomination unto Him in their life, but, in their death, they become His recompence.

The Lord is a spiritual as well as a natural Redeemer. He saves the germ-soul in each kingdom; He makes it possible for *all* to attain unto celestial life: but, upon evil He has pronounced an eternal curse,—it is death to the soul. "Every soul that sinneth, it shall surely die." "Why will ye die, oh! house of Israel? I would have saved you, but ye would not come unto me that ye might have life." Herein is the free-will of man made apparent;—the house of Israel chose death rather than life. "What shall it profit a man if he gain the whole world, and lose his own soul?" Indefinite language may be variously interpreted: it does not here say that a man shall not live, having lost his soul, but, what shall it profit him? that is, it shall profit not even the natural indulgence of his evil propensities, for they must perish with his soul. "Many sorrows shall be unto the wicked." But are there not many sorrows unto the righteous? Does virtue exempt the soul from suffering? The good man suffers, likewise the evil man. "The righteous perish, and no man layeth it to heart, none considering that he is taken from the evil to come." These words are mightily significant; they are our bulwarks, supporting our whole edifice,—that which we are now in process of erecting. The righteous are taken away from the evil to come, which no man considers to be the case. The inward life is hid with God, the outward life appears in the world. The evil man can no more do good and walk uprightly than the good man can do evil: both are under an influence over which they have no control. Now, if such were not the case, there would be no freedom of will; for if the good man knew that he must needs be good, he would have no incentive to virtue, no alliance would be formed with good in preference to evil, but he would be a mere machine acting as impelled by a power above its own order of creation. Therefore, the good man does not know, in the kingdom of nature, that with which he is perfectly conversant in the kingdom of spirit; for every son of Adam will acknowledge that he is not good interiorly, but that he is preserved from the exercise of his inherent evils by power from on high. But, if he be told that he is a wicked man, he dissents, considering himself unjustly condemned. This is not the case with the evil man: he does not allow that he is good either in nature or spirit; he knows that he is evil, but does not care to become otherwise; he does not like the company of the good, they are a restraint and a trouble to him,—he cannot associate with them any more than they can with him. So, conditions are equal; for neither desire the company of the other. Communion of interest does, however, exist; the good man is seeking life, and the evil man is seeking life; but one looks far on into eternity, the other looks not beyond the day in which he lives,—life to him is confined to the span in which he may indulge his inherent evils. Herein is prophecy. The wicked *know, interiorly*, that they are not immortal *in that state:* their acts prove it; they are never terrified into restraint; it cannot be, for the inner consciousness makes no response to any threat. They cannot hear the denunciations of the just; the inner ear does not hear the sound of their voice,—it falls upon the natural organ only; they go their way; nevertheless, God careth for them; His sun is ever shining for them as well as for the upright; they are very crooked and distorted in the spirit. If we see any one who is so in the body, how ready our sympathy! how tender our pity! What is it that we should waste a tear upon it? What is the body to the soul? "Fear not him who can destroy the body, but fear Him who can destroy both soul and body in hell, where their worm dieth not, and the fire is not quenched." This is the description of hell given by our Lord. In that hell the worm of evil dieth not, it feedeth on the soul, the flame of hell-fire is not quenched. So long as the evil spirit lives, so long must its torment endure,—so long must there be "weeping and gnashing of teeth." So long as there is evil in man or spirit whereby it can be nourished, so long does it continue to subsist. The good as well as the wicked man is under restraint in nature on account of evil, and suffers more or less according as his state determines; and so the fire is not quenched, and the worm dieth not, nor ever can, so long as the present order of life continues. This is the hell to which every scriptural passage alludes. Nature hath within a worm that cannot die. But after death, natural *and spiritual*, there is life for ALL; there is *manhood* for the race; there is everlasting purity and peace, and there is likewise everlasting punishment; for "every soul that sinneth, it shall surely die," and "every soul that sinneth not, it shall surely live, and not die." Are there *any* who sin not? If any man can lay his hand upon his breast and say, "I am sinless," he shall not only save his soul alive, but he shall redeem his body from the grave of dust and ashes; these witness against him that such an one would be a liar.

The contemplation of Gospel history is now essential to our progress towards that holy mount whereon we are to behold the Lord Jesus Christ transfigured before us; and it is not only His Spirit that is to assume a resplendence of aspect never before discernible, but His bodily development is to be seen in the light of *interior* nature to which our eyes are already partially open. In this light we behold nature resplendent with divine effulgence, and glorified in a manner that has never been previously presented to the view of humanity; and it has to be introduced with caution, for the eyes of mortals are weak, and they are very tremulous when elevated into regions above ordinary life. We are now leading them into unfrequented paths, and the earthly one they have hitherto trod must be henceforth regarded as the circuitous route by which the childhood of man has to be led up to the mountain summit of celestial knowledge. Men are busy with their several earthly avocations, and know not that which is passing in their soul's sanctuary, for they have not the inner eye open to see withal, nor the ear open to detect the sound of the axe, hammer, and saw which are daily plied to build up a temple fit for immortal spirits to dwell in.

The Lord is now in His holy temple, it is one not made with hands; within its walls there is silence; nature gives no heed—makes no sign. The days of John's sojourn in the wilderness are past. He is come again, verily, "this is Elias which was for to come." John the Baptist is truly risen from the dead; it is he whom the Herod of the world has beheaded; he is with Jesus, in His glory he is glorified; in His life Moses and Elias live; they met in

Christ, speaking with Him "of His decease which He should accomplish at Jerusalem." Moses drew Elias to the mountain summit on which he could alone meet the Lord. Elias had previously only done so in the wilderness where he baptized the people. Herein is much significance. But as we desire not to propound riddles requiring the aid of the spirit to solve, we shall, on this page, simply state that Moses is a man of the spirit as well as Elias. The age in which such can live is very different to that we now draw natural breath in. All things have changed. The former heavens and the former earth have passed away, and all things have been made new. In respect of nature, this prophecy was fulfilled before it was uttered. Nature is the prophet of spirit, and spirit is the prophet of nature. Thus the Lord conversed with Moses as He had formerly done on the Mount of Ascension. It was now Moses who descended to meet the Lord; beforetime the Lord descended to meet Moses, and to commune with him; in either case, the mountain height must be the place of meeting.

Communion with Deity can only be sustained under certain conditions of mind, and if we desire to be concise in our expression of truth, we say, that it is by ascending the mountain a man must prepare to meet his God. Thus it is that the Scriptures are written; they treat not of natural events in natural language, but they do treat of spiritual facts in natural language. They are, at this day, called to account for that in which they have no part. They are judged by men, when they treat not of the things of which men are cognizant. The Holy Scriptures are hidden treasures of which the present generation know nothing. They treat not of temporal matters, and are not fashioned after the manner that belongs unto natural life. They are spiritual not natural histories.

The Holy Scriptures are, however, standing upon a natural foundation, and if that is weakened by the substitution of a spiritual foundation, the fall of revelation is inevitable; for, what does the word imply but something which must be revealed to man, and man is natural as well as spiritual. It must be understood, that nature does not merely subsist in the present world, but is just as dominant after physical dissolution, as before it takes place. This is a very prominent point of observation, and unless it be kept in view, no knowledge can be gained of any spiritual theme. Nature is not spirit, neither is spirit nature; there is much distinction: but there is an earthly, and there is a spiritual manifestation of natural life; one is within the other. At death a man leaves the body of nature, and enters into the spirit of nature.

Moses is not to be considered a merely natural man. The account of his ascension of Mount Sinai is perfectly true *in the spirit*, pertaining to the world of *interior nature*, to which his acts are entirely referable. This statement may be substantiated, but not in few words. The scribe must write on, till more light can stream from her spiritually-directed pen; and it is only by patiently allowing it to move over the page, keeping her own mind as blank as that page previous to any written impression being made upon it, that any light can illuminate either the one or the other. The mind has so long and so reverently dwelt upon the literal text of scripture, and it is considered such sacrilege to interfere with it, even by substituting the more sacred facts of the spirit, that it is hard for any one professing so to do, to gain a patient hearing; nevertheless, we will speak and write, though the age may pass without giving heed to our proceeding. Blessings are sent in a day, but many days may pass ere they are appropriated.

These things shall now be much clearer explained; for, if we have to anticipate objections, and to temper expressions to the sensitive organ of nature, we shall never obtain a true and perfect note on that instrument which God has Himself placed in our hands. We are working one within the other; nature and spirit are in this work enlisted. Natural effect is produced by the operation of natural law, and spiritual effect by the operation of spiritual law; but there is an exquisite balance. The scale is equal, it does not oscillate.

I have said that knowledge is progressive: it is eminently so in respect of spiritual knowledge. The natural mind is discursive, it will wander in its way to the throne of God; it will cast its eyes hither and thither in search of mental food by the way-side. It likewise requires rest as well as change of diet, and it becomes weary. Then is the plane of operation uneven, and the various spiritual objects set upon it will not stand on a true level. But I have a spiritual mind whereon to place my objects, so they are undisturbed by the action of the lesser mind; that may, if it seem good unto it, so disport itself as a little child while its elders are conversing on subjects too high for the little one to comprehend; only, it must be obedient and quiet, that it offer no hindrance to the development of spiritual themes. This is the case with the writer of these words: she is desirous to promote the object of this work, but knowing not how to do so, she places herself in my spiritual company, giving up the reins of her mind into the hand of God, that He may lead her whither it shall seem good unto Him. My spiritual part in this proceeding has been already described, and needs no further explanation. It may, however, be again reverted to on a future page.

The love of Christ being universal, He saves all. The *desire* for salvation is not universal, for the evil do not care about it; they are in the death-slumber; they are dead as Lazarus when he had lain four days in the cave of the rock, and was like to stink. The

Lord said, "Lazarus is dead." This phrase is predicable of the spirit as well as of the body, and we find that sleep is likewise predicable of both; for the Lord said, "Lazarus sleepeth, but I go to awaken him out of sleep. The disciples say unto Him, Lord, if he sleep, he shall do well; but Jesus spake of the sleep of death." Death is unto the wicked, sleep unto the good. Stephen fell asleep: he is typical of the just,—past, present, and to come. The Lord made application of both states to Lazarus; he, it would appear, both slept and died; he was awakened out of sleep, and he was also raised from death unto life. He did not then " stink," as was supposed, but having lain in a grave " four days," his body must needs have done so. Doubtless, natural sense would have been offended by the contiguity of so loathsome a spectacle as the dead man would have presented to the eye of nature. But it was not seen, not perceived by any natural sense; it was only surmised that such would be the effect had it been exposed to observation.

But, the point to which I am leading is *not* discernible in the speech of Mary, but in that of our Lord. He said, " Lazarus is dead :" then, He addressed nature. He also said, " Lazarus sleepeth :" He then addressed spiritual perception within nature. The Lord thus spake on all occasions of addressing His disciples and others; but on the present occasion this duality of speech is particularly observable. The dead Lazarus was also the living Lazarus : the dead

G

man slept; the wicked ever do sleep; they are asleep, yet awake; alive, yet dead; and, if we may so venture to affirm, they are good, yet evil. "How is that possible?" cries affrighted nature. "How can it be otherwise?" observes the spirit of inward Adam, "seeing I was made by God into His own image and likeness, and God has Himself told us that all things which He made were 'very good?'" The deduction hence to be drawn is, that all nature is, all men are, still "very good," but that outwardly they are *very bad;* for, "there is *no man* good, no, not one;" or, to modify the expression, no man is as good as he was created. Then is the whole plan of redemption frustrated; for Christ came not to call the righteous, but sinners, to repentance,—to save the lost sheep of the house of Israel. The Lord Christ came to do that. Has He done it? If there be one sheep "lost," will He not seek for it and lead it back to the fold, and there will be more joy over that lost one found than over ninety and nine just persons who needed no repentance? But these just ones were not good, for no man is so; they were not evil, they did not commit sin; but as Adams they had one and all partaken of the forbidden fruit given them by their respective Eves. Thus they had fallen, and needed a Saviour as well as did "the lost sheep of the house of Israel." Without the redemption effected by Christ can no man see eternal life.

The Genesis narrative is not a fable of man's invention; it is God's fable wherewith to instruct

His children; it is now expounded in the ears of those who think they have found flaws in the Divine record of God's dealings with the children of men; who have themselves no knowledge of the path through which they can alone ascend up on high to meet their God. It is in nature that God must be met; natural minds must meet God as well as spiritual minds; all classes, all grades of intellect, all ages of human development must meet God, must meet Him in nature. Struggle and strife goes on, purity and impurity embrace, good and evil motive lead equally to action. Pride and humility, ignorance and knowledge, wisdom and folly,—all and each combine to work together in the production of effects that are wrought out from causes existing in the mind of Deity.

God does not make and unmake, neither does He allow man the power to unmake or remodel himself. Man cannot change one hair of his head from black to white, how then can he make himself evil when God has made him " very good?" Nature may, however, alter the aspect of creation; and that she does so is very apparent. Evil men are natural men, good men are spiritual men; spiritual principles are eternal, natural principles are temporary. Temporal life pertains to good men as well as to evil men. In nature there are sweet as well as bitter herbs, but the Scripture informs us that every herb of the field was good for food, and that they were all growing in heaven before they were placed upon the earth.

Poisonous herbs must then have been putting forth leaf and branch in heaven. It is so said in accordance with natural perception, which indicates the existence of good and evil habits in the same individual. The same mind that is virtuous in one sense, is not so in another. A man may be possessed of high and refined principles, but he may be very unamiable in natural disposition; he may be very covetous, and yet very generous; he may be very religious, and yet very irreligious: he is a bitter herb growing in heaven,—a plant in which there is health-restoring quality, but still it is poisonous. Thus every man is in the image and likeness of God, but he is in nature born into sin and conceived in iniquity, hence he is evil; there is no exception, because the birth into nature is identical with the birth into sin. Death is nature's release; the natural man dies, the spirit of nature perishes; it is in the grave in the cave of the rock; it is the stench of Lazarus which is there left; and when Lazarus comes forth, he is as though he had never seen corruption, for he is as he was before it commenced.

The man Lazarus is a spiritual-natural man, such as are all men. He had been sick, and he died, but that was unto nature, not unto spirit. He died bodily, not spiritually; he was clothed with mortal flesh, so he parted with it, never again to resume it; but he arose in natural life, and was visible and tangible, and sat with the Lord and the rest at supper. Did Lazarus do so, again coming into the nature in which and to which he had died? Verily, if so, the bird of prey would be uncreated, for they are made to feed upon carrion, and they would have been made dependent upon spirit instead of upon nature for their daily sustenance. The object of this allusion is to shew that not one of nature's laws can, by miracle, be infringed without an entire rupture of the whole order of terrestrial economy. No fowl could again fly across the firmament, if one particle of human flesh were to be rescued from decomposition. Every thread of life, natural and spiritual, is interwoven, one within the other; and if any flaw occur, any withdrawing from the texture, the whole will unravel and fall to pieces. As it was, Lazarus arose in the spirit of natural life; he died, and was buried; he stank, he polluted the atmosphere; at the grave his body did so, even while he sat at meat with the Lord of life.

The Lord loosed the bonds of nature when He said, crying with a loud voice, "Lazarus, come forth." It was the same when He said, "Talitha cumi,—Damsel, I say unto thee, Arise." These natural resurrections are not understood: they embody all that can be conveyed to the mortal mind in respect of spiritual resurrection,—from the grave of evil, from debased human nature, to life and righteousness, to eternal purity and peace; to more, to glory and dominion over the beast of the field, the fowl of the air, and the fish of the sea; to the inheritance of subjugation of the entire earth. This is the resurrection of the just: they rise to the primeval glory for which Adam was created. The just are Adam, the unjust are likewise Adam. There are not two Adams, but one; and man, be he good or be he evil, is Adam.

There are not various orders of human beings: all spiritual beings are as one man in the sight of God, and they are all in His image and likeness; not so exteriorly, but interiorly they are so. This one man, —this type of humanity, is saved by the advent of Jesus. He has saved the lost; He has raised the dead—body, soul, and spirit; He has done this in nature, but in so doing, He violated no natural law, —no spring has been disarranged, or even re-arranged, to suit the occasion. All has proceeded as though no miracle had ever taken place. A miracle does not imply any disarrangement of natural law. The Lord was about to rise with His own natural body from the sepulchre, so He raised other natural bodies.

The effect of the raising of Lazarus, also that of other dead persons, is not appreciable in nature as at present constituted; for, in the Gospel, as well as in the Genesis age, the world was in a very different state of interior spiritual perception to what it is at present. Then, Gospel truth could be immediately verified to the natural senses, which could be stimulated in a manner not at present possible; but there is evidence of a return to that primitive state being possible, and in a future age this statement will be universally received as truth. The borders of the land of Canaan are becoming visible, but the interior of that land cannot yet be reached.

The Genesis history is true; it is so as it appears to the perception of spiritual beings, for they view it with the enlightened eye of Adam, before the temptation and fall. The inner man does so even while he is clothed in flesh. The translations of the Bible may be incorrect, or may vary; that is of no account, the spirit remaineth whole and entire. The discrepancies of it are likewise of no import; they do but indicate the subserviency of nature to spirit; they are wholly referrible to the spirit, by means of which the literal narrative is compiled. The Holy Spirit is the author of every sentence. Had it been otherwise, no discrepancy could have occurred, no incongruity of fact been recorded, but a perfectly natural and harmonious description of events would have been given. The Holy Scriptures are not natural productions, hence in nature they are deficient. They are a divine expression as the Word of God. The natural man cannot discover the evidence that is so conspicuous to the spiritual mind; hence confusion and error: the disciples are not agreed among themselves; contention is leading them all into the right path; they are mutually enlightening each other. The Word of God is unharmed by these natural assailants; it is parting with its garments to one and to another, and presently, men will see it come forth in its own naked purity and holy truth. But so long as there is sin, and so long as Adam is ashamed of his own form, that which God has made him in, so long must Bible revelation be covered with a natural clothing, and it is so marred and despoiled by the dust of earth that it is hardly recognizable as the Divine Word of truth to man. These things are mysterious; no man may say wherefore they are so, neither does he know how they can ever be otherwise, neither does any angel, but God only.

The inward Adam of whom mention has been made, is not discrete from the outer man, but is ever at variance with him. The strife of tongues identified with the builders of Babel, is ever going on within the soul. The good man hears its clamour as well as the bad man. This state of mental experience is the Adam of nature striving with the Adam of spirit: the error of all doctrine, the contrariety of all feeling subsisting even between the most righteous persons, is the strife of inward with outward Adam. The hope of the good is for peace and for truth; in the world, it is very rarely attainable. The outward Adam is silenced, the inward dominant.

This state is indicated by the history of Lazarus: he represented man naturally developed as are all other men; but the Lord made it appear that all are internal as well as external, even in natural life. All men are Adam. Throughout these pages it is to be noted that the term "Adam" refers to *all* men; likewise "Eve" applies to all women: whether a man be good, he is represented by "the man" or "Adam;" and whether a woman be good or evil, she is represented by "woman," or "Eve."

The wicked are made by God as they are; and the good are made as they are: and neither can alter the conditions of their birth from God, any more than a human babe can do so from its natural birth into the world. The evil must needs do evil, and the good must needs do good. But we must not be startled at this plain statement of a very evident truth. The righteous are not more favored by God than are the unrighteous, who cannot help being as they are: but they are "very sick," they are diseased,—offensive maladies are upon them; they are tended for these calamities in the hospital of souls. In the Bethlehem Sanctuary, there is a Physician never weary of attending to their plaints, to their imprecations, to their blasphemies, to their lies; for these things go up into His ears and draw forth the manifestation of His attributes more potently than the righteousness of the just; they are ever standing in His presence; but these unjust ones have to be called into that presence by a loud voice. The Lord is ever calling unto Lazarus to come forth of the grave where he stinketh; and when he is come forth, He taketh him home to sit at meat with Him. He who goeth about as a roaring lion seeking whom he may devour, is this same Lazarus,—the dead stinking Lazarus. The risen Lazarus is Adam redeemed, saved.

This is enigmatical speech to unspiritual ears; but it is the language in which inspiration ever speaks. The dead bury their dead. How is that? Christ is dead when He gives up the Ghost; Christ is risen when He comes forth of the sepulchre. Mary was His mother once, presently she is "woman." John is Elias and Elias is John. The same order of transformation takes place in the spirit, that is primary, the letter subservient. Nature is responsive to the cry of spirit: "Lazarus, come forth," is echoed from rock to valley, from plain to mountain height. Lazarus comes forth; the dead arise; they do so in nature. What! with the dead body revivified? No! they leave that in caves, in graves or in ocean beds, or in ashes. They feed the wolf and carrion bird of prey; but they do arise at the loud cry of Omnipotence; the dead arise; aye, from the grave, from forth that pollution bed, they come and go up to sit at meat with Him whose almighty call they have obeyed: and, when they so sit down in His kingdom, there are Israelites who would fain put them to a second death; for they think it more natural that the dead should remain dead. They who thus seek the life of risen Lazarus, seek also that of the Lord Himself, "Inasmuch as ye have done it unto the least of these my brethren, ye have done it unto me." Take heed then that we reject not unusual manifestations of truth; for we may be rejecting the Lord of Truth.

Lazarus was dead and is alive, was lost and is found: was buried and is risen from the grave. By what means? By the voice of Deity in nature. That cry has sounded in the ears of nature: it has vibrated on the breath of air we are now inhaling; we who yet live upon the earth are, at this moment, drawing breath in that atmosphere wherein stood Lazarus and Jesus, Mary, and the envious Jews: we think of the lapse of time since then; true, states have changed; many have lived and died since then; epochs have passed and left no trace of their existence; countless ages have passed, or a moment, an hour or a day, which is it? No man may say: the answer is, To one it is an age, to another, It was so done an hour since. Mind is the bridge of time; mind is progressive, fathomless: it is illimitable. Nature is coeval with Deity. There is no time,—no nature possible before God, neither can anything come into existence after He is; for He is not progressive, as is His creation, consequently He is all in all; He possesses all—past, present, and future, in Himself. Man is not receptive of all states in one coeval experience; he is therefore creative to himself: man divests himself of one state, and puts on another; then, he is conscious of the lapse of time; he calls change of state time.

Christ called forth the dead Lazarus; He did so by the utterance of a loud cry in nature. The same effect would have followed His whisper, but He spake and acted, not for Himself but for others,—for those who stood by: these would have heard His speech just as well had it been low as being loud. The Lord was a natural as well as a divine man. He pleaded for nature, for He knew her requirements; He was in nature then, is He less so now? Natural sight beholds Him not; the eye of the spirit sees Him standing at the mouth of the cave: and it hears the loud cry, and it sympathizes in the grief of the afflicted sisters. But it does not understand the scene: it knows not in what body the dead arise, or how they come: that consciousness is closed; it was not open in any one of the gazers upon the risen man. He came forth bound in grave-clothes hand and foot. Jesus said, "Loose him; let him go free;" yet, the body lay still bound in the cave of the rock. Yea, this is truth; the world will laugh Jesus to scorn even when He saith, "The maid is not dead, but sleepeth." Neither laughter nor crying can affect us: we speak of that we do know, and we may not cease our utterance, save at the mandate of God.

Lazarus had fallen sick,—had died and was buried; he stank and could by no means be restored to life and light. But his prison-bars could be unloosed; his grave-clothes unbound: not so, in the nature to which he had expired; he had ceased to breathe natural air; he had ceased to need it. Where was his life,—his spirit? In the body that stank, or in that body which has no natural particle to stink? That *spiritual* body in which Adam, or man, is created free from sin, before being conceived in iniquity: *that* body retained the life of Lazarus: that was the man called forth by Christ. That it could subsist in debased human company is not surprising, when we consider that man was, *in nature,* made a "living soul;" that it was the Lord God who did so make man before death and the grave came into existence. In that presence man could again become a living soul, just as if death had never been; bearing in mind, that time has no place in the transactions of Deity. God is God, whether manifest in the person of Jesus Christ or not. He did not either lose or gain by that divine manifestation; being the same yesterday, to-day, and for ever.

It was then the "living soul" of Lazarus that came forth of the grave; yet bound about with grave-clothes. Marvellous admixture of nature and spirit! *Clothes* then adhered to the spirit of the risen one, though flesh did not! When the dead arise, will they come in shrouds? In what bodies will they come? They are with the living now, they are standing at your side while you read this book; they are in your life; that is their body of nature; they are in the sight of your mental eye: that is their vestment. *You* are clothing the dead; *you* are bringing them up from the grave, in the bodies you loved to see them in on earth; and though they do not come before your mental vision in grave-clothes, still they do so come in earth-garments. Jesus at the sepulchre was clothed in a garment that made Mary think she saw the gardener. What gardener could have removed the body of Jesus, that she should say, "Sir, if thou hast borne Him hence, tell me where thou hast laid Him, and I will take Him away?" Could she so speak, believing that the man she saw had so done? or if so, how could the stone be rolled away? Natural sequence is at fault; spiritual perception is consecutive; spiritual perception instructed Mary at the holy sepulchre, that Jesus was the Gardener of souls. She saw not Jesus as she had known Him in life; but she saw Him as her spirit told her He truly was. She is the Mary of to-day; she, woman, is still weeping at the grave of Lazarus, and at the sepulchre of Christ; she does not yet know that her brother can be saved, nor that her Lord is risen. She knows that at the last day, the dead arise at the call of Omnipotence, and at the presence of Deity in the flesh. But Jesus did not bring forth His linen clothes, nor His head-napkin; He had disturbed them, had removed them from His sacred form, but left them unaffected by the office they had fulfilled for Him: He clothed Himself in the garments of "the gardener." Jesus so appeared to Mary by virtue of an inward impression made upon her spirit, of which she was not outwardly conscious. She spake from an interior consciousness of truth, which also caused her to see the Lord as the "gardener." This statement may not be apprehensible to every one, but by patient investigation into the case of Lazarus, in connection with that of the Lord's resurrection from death and the sepulchre; we shall presently behold that which will enable us to comprehend the scriptural text, in a clearer light than it has yet appeared in.

The world is incredulous; it believes not in the power, by means of which this utterance is effected,— that does not hinder its utterance; it only alters the mode of its development; it compels us to avoid being too explicit in dealing with the matter, for if the whole truth be at once divulged, no man will stand by to hear; they will one and all walk out of the temple, leaving Christ and the woman alone, to be instructed by His divine speech.

This is an illustration of the power of vision, by which Mary Magdalene could alone behold the Lord. She could be indrawn into the interiors of natural life; then she saw Jesus as the gardener, whom she thought might have borne Him hence. She knew not what she said, any more than the awe-struck Peter, on the mount. She was then a "living soul" in nature; the bodily sense was closed, it was as though it had never been opened; yet she wept and mourned,—she thought of Jesus as He had been, not as He was; she did not think of grave-clothes, save in connection with the body; and she had seen them all lying in the sepulchre by themselves and the napkin that had bound His head lying apart by itself; so she did not expect to find even the Lord's body clothed; yet she thought the gardener might have borne Him hence, and she might fetch Him away. Her vision took the form of her interior mind; had it been otherwise, she would have seen the body of the Lord still lying dead in the sepulchre. The male disciples had likewise seen but the linen garments, and when they journeyed to Emmaus, they were blind equally with Mary, whose report they did not credit. But their state and that of Mary was very different. The present object can only be obtained by a comparison between the case of Mary Magdalene at the holy tomb, and that of the congregation at the grave of Lazarus; both receptacles for the dead were in the caves of rocks. Who shall say that Jesus lay where no man had previously done, and not Lazarus also? It is not usual to remove dead bodies from the last resting-place, yet stress is laid upon this particular. The grave is a rock in both cases: in one it is a cave, in the other it is a new sepulchre hewn out of the rock. Why this peculiarity? It is not unnecessary to note these things, for our theme is entirely based upon them.

Scrupulosity of diction is remarkable throughout the Scripture records; they are so constructed as to bear a double and a treble interpretation. Bible version is prophetic; it is of no relative account that translations differ, or that learned criticism finds numerous flaws in the text; the fact of its being the popular version, read in the churches, preached from, committed to memory, is quite sufficient to prove its value; it has so lived and so worked upon the hearts of men; and had it been more correctly translated than it is, the effect must have been different; and in the Almighty councils it was not desired and not intended to be different to that it has been. In this view then we take the holy text as it stands, not as it might have been by the learned more correctly translated; with that we have nothing to do. When the time has come for a more correct version to be given to the unlearned, they will be in a position to receive a higher order of truth than they are yet able to appreciate.

Mary at the tomb of Christ and Mary at the grave of Lazarus were under an equal influence; they were one and the same; the Magdalene had sinned and was forgiven, the Mary had wept twice over Christ. He wept for her brother, she thrice wept: for herself, for her brother, and for Christ. She, the weeping one, is the type of woman—the Eve—Mary—the severed one—the shunned of pharisaical pride—yet finding access into his house; seeking for her Lord at the feast of nature; wiping His feet with her hair; sitting at His feet to catch His words; leading Him to the sepulchre of her dead brother; bending over the sacred tomb; looking in, her tears again falling, where He had lain; bearing to men the first report of His resurrection and presence in nature. This is the mission of woman; she is ever following in the steps of the Magdalene. She is doing all that this Mary did: she is the sinner and the saint; the evil and the good; the impure and the chaste. The Lord called "Mary." She turned and knew Him; but He said, "Touch me not, for I am not yet ascended to my Father. Go tell the brethren." The analogy is here perfect. Mary was not aware that her brother could rise from death in nature; she thought He would do so at the last day. Neither did the Magdalene think that the Lord could raise Himself from the dead; she thought to find His body still dead in the tomb. She was not so ignorant in the spiritual degree of her life; if she had been, she would have seen the Lord as He was at last seen of her; but she both spake and saw by virtue of a perception that fell into nature, yet did but partially enlighten the merely natural senses. She was aroused by the call "Mary;" then she knew the Lord; for, be it observed, she turned *back* before she could do so. Her eyes were again opened *upon nature*, they turned from inward to outward nature, and she knew the Lord, for He then appeared to her as she had been used to see Him. This is also the case with Mary at her brother's grave; she thought to see a dead man; but here she was under a different influence, she had not come out to see the dead Christ, but the living Christ; she knew His power in nature, "Lord, if Thou hadst been here, my brother had not died." But she knew that He could not raise up dead bodies, so she went with distrust to the grave, for she said "by this time he stinketh." Yea, so he did: he stinketh even now, for time is of no avail to remove it; it is an everlasting stench that dead men send up into the nostrils of Deity. But He does not heed it, for He is come to save them; to draw forth the spiritual body out of that polluted grave; it comes forth at His call, and at His call, Mary knows her Lord.

The object of the Lord's suffering throughout His natural life, and His subsequent death, was to save the lost—the evil beings who had grievously offended against His holy laws. Those who were doing so in the earth-life were as a drop in the ocean, compared with those who were preparing to do so in the spirit; and when these last should be born, there would be no present Saviour to rescue them from eternal destruction, if Christ had not effected His advent into nature at the time, and in the manner that He did. But these unborn spirits were not in nature; they could not be affected by any divine manifestation *then* taking place in a condition of life they had not entered upon and had no affinity with. These also are "the lost sheep of the house of Israel" Jesus came to save; for them He wept and groaned, was crucified and died, arose from the sepulchre whole and entire. But in the life to come there must be suffering for every soul that sinneth, and death *must* supervene on every malignity that is perpetuated there. One crime is enough; it is not necessary to enumerate convictions there; one tendency to sin will vitiate the springs of spirit existence. The lamp of life will flicker, exhaust itself, and finally become extinct; it has died the death of the wicked. Is there no resurrection—no life unto the *spirit?* Christ has brought life and immortality to light; He has walked forth of the sepulchre, therefore shall every spirit do so too; Christ died the death of the wicked, *not* the death of the righteous, and He did so that *the wicked* might follow Him. The righteous need not die, they "shall never die;" but those who die shall live in Him. He came, not to save the righteous, but to call sinners to repentance; and repent they must, even because that was the object of His advent into nature. The Lord has opened the gate of life, and every bound soul may now go free, they do all "stink," but that does not interfere with their resurrection unto life and righteousness; they shall, one and all, sit at meat with Christ their Saviour.

The Lord is a divine Parent, consequently so soon as the evil life is extinct as to manifestation, it returneth unto Himself, it is then breathed forth of His essences, and it goes out from His life into the life of His creature woman; but she is a dependent creation, she cannot hold her life separate from that of man, so the interior soul-Adam that resides in every feminine member, is a parent, responding to the divine action by means of which it is preserved from outward pollution, and the resuscitated spirit-life is born again into the *interiors of nature*, the plane on which it died. It is made a spiritual Adam, it is registered in *outward* life as the "mighty men," "men of renown" that were of old. These heroes are lost souls, resuscitated devils—maniacs, whom Christ has restored to their right minds, fed and clothed. These be they who have come again into the womb of woman, having angelic fathers not after the flesh but after the *inward spirit*, born from the *essences* of nature, not from the dross of its outer garment. These be the "lost sheep" restored to the fold—the mighty company of purified souls clothed in white, pure and clean. The just are made perfect, but not by death,—not by the experience of the unjust; they are purified, purged with hyssop, and made whiter than snow; but they love the process, they know its need; they submit to the tending of spirit-physicians, and they themselves assist in the work that is to effect their final liberation from every earthly bond. *These* shall "never die," they have put on immortality in nature, and it shall in no wise be taken from them; they have on the wedding garment of righteousness. But the evil had none given them to put on. No! it was kept from them that it might not be defiled, for there is but one for each, and if that be polluted, there is none other. So the Lord kept it in His own wardrobe, that it might be ready to put on when the "outer court" had done its work.

The fact of man being born into the world an infant implies his declension, which necessitated the advent of Christ as an infant also, in order to effect man's redemption; He had redeemed the spiritual man in Eden-life, He now descended to redeem man in nature. He followed him; He came down to dwell among the "lost sheep" of whom He was the

Shepherd; He dwelt among them as one of them; He remained under the cloud of sin till it should be dispersed by the splendour of the Sun. When that should shine forth, every soul would be saved. Not till then could any divine light appear around His holy head. Jesus rested on the arm of flesh; He brought Himself into that juncture in which eternal death must ensue, if the conditions on which eternal life can alone be sustained be not drawn forth into nature. This was the agony and the cause of the blood-sweat. All was lost, all was vanquished by the powers of the air. The darkness of nature could not otherwise have occurred. All *was* lost; the kingdom of light and righteousness had been invaded, it was given over to destruction and death. Jesus gave up the ghost, in nature He did so; but the darkness was dispelled; light again dawned upon the earth, and this *before* Jesus came forth of the sepulchre. He left no stone before His sepulchre; He rolled back every obstacle to the restoration of the race to their primitive endowments. He not only conquered hell and death, but He allowed them to conquer Him; then He wrested the palm of victory from out their hand, and bore it through the sepulchre, through the stone and through the rock; and more, through the flesh of fallen man. He saved His persecutors and His revilers; He restored *them* to their lost inheritance; He reversed conditions with them; He put on their filthy garments, and interwove them with His own robe of righteousness; and by so doing He made them whiter than snow in Salmon. Jesus took upon Himself the condition of the *lost*. He took upon Himself the estate of man *without the counterpart*. Man, under that condition, must needs do evil, must become a devil and no man. All the evil, without exception, are in that position; they have no helpmeet in nature. A wife taken after the custom of the world, is not such a helpmeet as God made for man before he was born into natural life. The true helpmeet is a spiritual-natural partner. The wicked are not provided with any such partner, and the consequence is, that they cannot sustain life of any spiritual degree; they can but move through the world as human animals, but are not men save in externals; they have all the requisites for perfection, but these are not developed into nature. The Lord personified every degree of human life; no human entity but is perfectly represented in His divine Person. All benefit by His advent into nature; but *the lost*, these are His peculiar charge; their nature He assumes; their condition He is born into; their salvation He effects. By birth from Mary, He inducts Himself into her parentage, that of a sin-begotten ancestry. But this subject is of very intricate bearing: the mind must ever be at fault trying to comprehend that which is above its mortal grasp.

The Lord comes to take into Himself that principle of humanity which causes death; for it pertains to all. The good man dies as to his body, likewise the little child. The innocent are like unto the guilty in the matter of death. The pure in heart can alone see God; they see Him, and they shew Him forth to the view of others in their lives. To the froward God shews Himself froward. God is seen under every possible aspect; for, as to His Divine Humanity, He is in man. Weakness is apparent in the life of Christ; infirmity, sorrows, temptations, and every natural belonging, is recorded as pertaining unto Him; yet He is received as God; He is shewn to be almighty and creative, and possessing life in Himself. This should inform us that all our human belongings are in God : evil and suffering do not pertain unto Him as God; but these woes do pertain unto Him as man; that is, Jesus can take diseases into Himself without the manifestation of evil, but not without that of suffering. He suffers for the good man in the spirit; for the evil man He suffers in the body. For the man of sin He dies that he may die too; for the good man He lives, that he may live and not die. The cross is for murderers and thieves; they shall be with Him in Paradise; but, for their sins they suffer. "We are justly condemned; but what hath this man done?" All suffering cometh of evil; where there is no evil, no suffering can be experienced. That the innocent do undergo many natural pains, is undeniable; but who is innocent of the great transgression? who is irresponsible in spirit? The Lord suffered as man in the good state, and as man in the bad state. He, the Lord of life, having life in Himself, dies the *second death* with the murderer and thief.

The Lord is in our souls saving them; crucifying Himself in us; putting off flesh infirmity in us; raising us from the grave. We all die in Him that we may live in Him. The Lord is with every man; *in* every man, whether he be good or whether he be evil; but the manifestation of His divine presence is different in each, the manner of salvation diverse; as much so as is the exhibition of natural life. Hence the different phases in the Lord's life, as narrated in the New Testament. His suffering and death relate to the interior life of the good, and to the exterior life of the wicked. His almighty and creative power is relative to the exterior life of the good, His suffering and death to their interior life; for He is absorbing their interior evils into Himself that He may be crucified instead of them. The evil,—they who perish by the second death,—do likewise absorb into their spiritual essences the evils with which the good are interiorly infected, and they die the death of the spirit, in Christ, that the righteous may be thereby exempt. But the Lord is *in* man; these finite redeemers are without him. The divine Saviour comes to redeem *interior* humanity.

"The wicked shall be a ransom for the righteous, and the transgressor for the upright," (Prov. xxi. 18.) They are reservoirs into which the pollution of the whole world is cast; they take our sins, and bear our infirmities,—sustain the reproach and suffering due unto every soul that is not perfect before God.

The Gospel age is an ever present age; not one period of time more than another is Gospel age; every day is the day of Christ's advent into nature. My words are not prophetic, but are present testimonies to the truth of revelation. The Bible records are not compiled from ear or eye-witnesses; neither from report, or tradition; but from divine inspiration alone: they are written from inward dictate. If they are of any present utility, it must be by virtue of their present application to the race, and, therefore, be applicable to every individual member of the race, and must rest upon a foundation not laid in space and time. The Lord is ever present with His bride, the Church; if at one period, at all periods; yet, He is differently apprehended by each; all look upon Him with different eyes, and view Him under different aspects. The Lord would have them do so. In this respect we are distinctive from the Gospel historians; they representing their Lord and Master as natural as it is possible to be; yet combining in all their accounts of Christ, the divine element with the purely natural. This is the distinction we wish to note between our apprehension of Jesus and theirs: they were prone to divulge His *outward*, we His *inward* nature. The Gospels are essential to the life of Jesus in His Church. He must be outwardly as well as inwardly apprehended: and the outward reception must precede the inward, or there will be no foundation whereon to build it.

The Lord is in close conjunction with our souls; He is in our nature; this is indicated by the infirmity ascribed to Him. Christ is living in us, and likewise dying in us: the crucifixion is the portrayal of our condemnation in nature: we are all under the curse of sin; but still we cannot live a single moment independent of the life of Christ in us. The Gospel is emphatic on this head: the Lord's natural advent and crucifixion are essential to this end: no flesh can otherwise be saved. So He is crucified in all, whether good or evil. The Lord Jesus desires to be thus crucified; for, if we crucify Him not, He cannot save us. If we fight off the servants of the High Priest who have come out to take Him, He will reprove us; for He says, For this purpose came I into the world. But in this crucifixion act He suffers, His Humanity does so. What is the Humanity of Christ? It is the natural life we each hold in God; that is the Humanity of the Lord Jesus. He put it on Himself in Eden before man was born upon this earth. He shewed Himself to Adam and to Eve as a Divine Man. As we live in Christ so we must die in Christ; we must be partakers in His death as well as in His resurrection. His Humanity is our humanity, for we are dependent upon Him for our being, and for the power of motion. He represents all human consciousness; hence the extremity of suffering. In us it is apportioned according to our several states of distinct consciousnesses; but He is God, and to the Divine Being in Himself no affliction is possible; if there were, He could have no joy in the creation of man, who is in constant bondage to flesh infirmity. Man regards the Divine Being from the standpoint of nature, so he must needs see Him as a natural God; but when He is viewed from the standpoint of spirit, He is seen to be divine without any admixture of natural concomitant.

The Testaments are all of equal importance to mortals; equally life sustaining; fraught with divine wisdom adapted to the necessities of mankind. They are, in reality, but one Testament. It is not the present mission to interfere in any Biblical controversy that may, at this day, be agitating society. It is with interior verity that we are alone concerned: with intermediates we have no relation.

The Genesis account of creation is shewn to be a narration of ever present supernatural facts that are taking place every hour we live; and shall we be understood when we affirm that the Gospel narratives are no less *present* realities? Shall we enunciate a hard saying indeed, or shall we thereby render a hard saying easy of comprehension; placing the Gospel of Jesus upon a pinnacle from which all nations and kingdoms of the earth may behold their Lord and their God?

The Lord Jesus is our Redeemer, our divine Saviour from the lusts of the flesh and from the infirmities of nature. He has paid the penalty which we owe to God; He has come down from his high estate, has incarnated Himself into our nature, has led captivity captive, and vanquished hell and death. He has left no part of that work undone or imperfect. The Lord is a divinely incarnated man. When He appeared among men it was in the flesh of *interior*, not of exterior, human nature. He is our flesh Redeemer, but not our *bodily* Redeemer: had He made his advent to *that* extent, He would have raised all men even as Himself. But He came to redeem the lost, —to redeem the germ-soul, to cause woman to give it re-birth. It was essential to His advent that Mary should give Him birth, yet without the natural co-operation of Joseph. This birth would introduce Him into the *interiors of natural life,* but *not* admit Him into the *exteriors* of natural life. It would place Him in the position of lost or wicked souls; for, the necessity of His natural birth was, that it should effect this divine purpose. If it were only a spiritual birth that Mary could give Him, then He would not attain the life of nature which was so essential to the restoration of the race; therefore, the Lord came into Mary's natural life. He partook of her essences; He interfered with no natural arrangement; for he had Himself prepared the way

for His own descent into nature; He had so done
ere the prophetic announcement of His advent
reached the mortal ear. He prepared His hand-
maiden by withdrawing her from the person of Adam
in the Eden life. That act was the announcement of
His flesh advent. The Lord would take upon Himself our nature; but the woman that was called Eve
could not produce Him; she is still unable to do so.
Mary can give birth to the Lord, but not *Eve*. He
comes by virtue of no natural union with man, but is
born of an affianced virgin, such as are all women
interiorly; so soon as womanhood becomes apparent,
so soon is Eve become Mary. She is then able to perform the use for which she was severed from Adam,
and perform it she must, or else her natural life cannot be sustained. Mary is then to be understood in
the comprehensive sense of WOMAN. As all are Eves
so all are Marys. Natural feeling, ancestral prejudices may start back in affright at this announcement; but that does not hinder the progress of
interior truth. The Gospels are true, much more
true, much more divine in their origin and bearing
than any living man has any conception of. By
placing them upon a merely earthly foundation they
are desecrated, though unwittingly. The facts of the
Gospels are divine as well as natural. But, in the
mere earth-life they did never take place. The Lord
entered into the soul and into the body of Mary; the
power of the Highest overshadowed her; she—woman
—is the handmaid of the Lord; she can perform the

work He requires of her, that is, to redeem His people from their sins,—to give them one and all re-birth. In the performance of that involuntary act, she is giving birth to the Redeemer Himself; and it is by virtue of His divine presence that she can so carry out His beneficent designs in her separation from man. The resuscitating devil which, it has been said, is ever gestating in the womb of woman, is so, by virtue of the divine presence in and with this natural parent; it is the power of the Highest overshadowing her; it is the manifestation of the Divine Being in nature. He is said to have been born of Mary an infant, and the whole narration from birth to crucifixion and subsequent ascension is related in a perfectly circumstantial and consecutive manner; so that the evident impression of the writer was, that he, with truth and accuracy, chronicled a perfectly literal history of natural occurrences. And it was so intended to be received. No mistake has arisen; no false interpretation established; it has been received by mankind as the Lord intended it should be. But the Lord spake in parables, and without a parable spake He not unto them. He is now speaking in the interpretations of those same parables. He has impressed His servants the prophets to write of Him, and He has likewise impressed His servants the Evangelists to write of Him; and He has impressed His disciples in all past ages so to believe on Him. But, the obstacles in this path must be systematically met and cleared of every difficulty; if the present system of interpretation we have thus far entered upon carry not conviction of truth into every heart, it must be capable of doing so to some, and as it is supernaturally given forth, so must it be supernaturally received.

The Lord is ever with His people; to their low estate He adapts Himself: He is born into 'human nature in accordance with its capacity to receive Him. He is born of woman into her nature, but if that nature changes,—becomes more elevated in its capacities, then, is He not born again of that increased capacity? The Israelite is still anticipating his flesh advent: is Christ, then, unborn for him? nay; He is born of Jew and Gentile equally as of the Christian Mary. But are there no spiritual,—no celestial Marys who can also give the Saviour birth? There are: they are big with child; they are burdened with a creation which they cannot give natural birth to. The Saviour of souls is coming to the souls who require re-birth; they do all receive it from Him, for they are born of that feminine part which is in His undivided body. When we have truly put on Christ, we are no longer men and women. Of that nature which is undivided, comes the Christ; with Him comes the manifestation of presence, that is, womanhood; manhood is likewise in Christ, but not outwardly exhibited, that is, the Lord is not naturally born of man, but only so of woman. The Lord is man and woman, but in unity not in division. He is Adam, not Adam and Eve. Mary could be alone employed to give the Lord birth; but, that it might be subsequently understood *how* it was that she could do so, the Evangelists were impressed to make mention of one Joseph, her affianced husband. This man had no natural knowledge whatever of the part he was performing in the divine manifestation to which purpose Mary was called. But the text implies, that Mary was just as conscious of the birth of Jesus as of her other* sons, whose father was Joseph. The implantation of the germ-soul in the womb of woman, is not a conscious experience with any female; yet she does experience a very palpable effect upon its removal, which is a periodical occurrence "after the manner of women." This failure of natural consciousness in the conception of the germ-soul, is fraught with interior blessing, for if the parent were open to such a perception in nature, the consequences would be very disastrous to her state. The evils of which the resuscitating spirit had died in the hell of interior nature, would be a present perception to her, and under such conditions, she could not retain her own integrity: she must be kept in entire ignorance of all that daily occurs within the deep recesses of her own spirit; of that germinal conception her bodily senses must make no report; but, of the passing away of the natural clothing she is ever conscious, and it must needs be akin to child-birth into the world. That this manifestation should vary in individuals is not of any account, for every natural constitution is personally distinctive. The glance we are taking at the general sanitary law by which the physical constitution of woman is sustained, is sufficient for our purpose. Woman is formed for giving natural birth to offspring: man engenders them, she produces them. We have seen that the Lord made man equal to the performance of both, but he did not fulfil the command, to be fruitful and multiply; therefore, woman came forth of him, and in so doing, she gave birth to the Lord Christ, who appeared not unto Adam till Eve was in creation: neither did He make any personal appearance whatever till the pair had sinned. So soon as they required re-birth, so soon did the Lord God appear as man, walking, in scripture phraseology, in the garden at the close or cool of the day. Thus it was that Christ was dependent for His personal advent on the co-operation of woman; which would not have been needed had she not come forth of Adam; for, with woman came sin and infirmity into nature. With all evil development came the Lord Christ; He followed it step by step into the very earthlife; into every haunt of devilry, came He—the Lord Christ; for He came to save the lost,—to immortalize His own creation,—to neutralize the consequences of Adam's *inward* declension which, as has been shewn, was provided for by the birth of Eve. This Eve-woman is the incipient Mary; she is born into nature-Eve, but becomes Mary. Man is born Adam after the severance, but, when he is grown in wisdom and in stature, he becomes Joseph; and he does then *interiorly* affiance himself to the woman of his soul. Then comes the angel Gabriel and foretels to them both, though in diverse manner, the birth of the Lord Christ, who shall redeem His people from their sins. This enunciation is made in the spirit to the spirit; no woman hears it with her earthborn ear; no man dreams it in natural slumber. The visions of the night do not reveal divine verities that concern every mortal in existence; but the inner consciousness is awake; night or day it sleepeth not. Old things are new when first made known to us; so these present enunciations are revelations to the ear of nature only; the spirit ear is well accustomed to their utterance, and marvelleth not at such knowledge. The Lord is now revealing Himself to the natural comprehension of woman, in so far as it is possible at this day; but in another age this will be inadequate to meet its requirements, and every revelation will be, on its first announcement, regarded with extreme fear, caution, and distrust, as removing the foundations on which former times have rested.

The Lord is all in all to all men. Eve, the woman, was not in outward but in inward nature. Eve, the child, comes into outward earthly nature. Mary ever dwelleth in the presence of God; hence Gabriel is with her, for he needed not flight to bring him down to earth; he was with Mary, and together they stood in the presence of God, and left that presence not. Gabriel himself testified that he flew not down to earth, neither did he, in his visit to Mary, descend into any sphere less exalted than that he was ever accustomed to stand in: for he says, "I am Gabriel that stand in the presence of God." Now, herein is much perplexity to the natural comprehension; for Mary was more interior than Eve, and yet was in exterior whilst Eve was in interior conditions of natural life; and Eve produced, by inference, a Divine man, whilst Mary produced, by circumstantial account, a babe.

The germ-soul is extant in every phase of human life: it pervades the entire system of humanity; but nature is the culminating point of creation: every other stage of life is gradational; but, on the plane of nature—external earthly nature, is the ladder fixed, on which the angels of God are ever ascending and descending; they come down from their heaven of nativity, rest the foot on earth, and then they go up, *step by step*, even as they have come down. Hence it is that nature external is the plane on which the Lord will receive His human birth, and He will be so celestially, so interiorly born of woman, that she shall receive Him even as her earth-born sons into her womb; she shall give Him infantile nativity. But, to suppose that such a conception as the Lord Christ's could ever produce a babe with earthly concomitants, subject unto the gross requirements of mortal flesh, is to make Him a merely earth-born man with spiritual God-like endowments, but with no *natural* deification whatever. God is man in nature, but Jesus, as received by professing Christians, is no more God than other men. He performed miracles, which are not cognizable to the natural senses. He multiplied food, but the essences were in the interiors of nature, from whence did the substance then proceed?

The Gospels are a consistent whole, they are not relative to physical nature in one part, and to spiritual nature in another part. The ascension to the pinnacle of the temple is just as much a literal fact as that which took place in the air after the crucifixion. It is all applicable to the states of individuals; and as they are, at the present stage of existence, under the law of divided consciousness, so the Lord is represented as being born of one, received by another, denied, crucified, loved, scorned, and rejected, revered or blasphemed in every stage of His course through nature, which means the inner consciousness of different orders of His finite creature-man. But, that this thing be more clearly elucidated, we will take an instance from the experience of any one member of the Lord's Church on earth. In infancy or childhood, the Lord is very differently regarded by us to what He is in after-life: in adolescence, He is growing in wisdom and in stature; in manhood, He is seen as the Redeemer in the natural sense of that term; in old age, He is still differently appreciated. Again, in states of sickness, mental perplexity and affliction, in joy and exultation, in repentance and remorse, in humiliation, despair, degradation and anguish, supplication, prayer or praise and thanksgiving—in all these several conditions of the human mind, the Lord Jesus is variously contemplated. In adaptation to the various necessities of mankind was the Gospel narrative compiled.

The Lord could not come into the outer flesh-clothing of woman, for it will not contain spiritual much less Divine seed. The covering put on by our Lord was spiritual, or the body of *inward* nature—this is the law of spiritual maternity; it came into existence with woman, and unless she can obey it she cannot live in the world; consequently, the Lord may be said to have had birth from woman in the world, for it is there that law comes into operation, and on no other plane is it operative. The Lord was born as are the lost souls; their germ-soul is re-born of woman, but not into the earth of our external existence; it is essential to His purpose of redemption that He touch not that plane of merely animal human life, for, by so doing, sexual division would be at once abolished, and the purpose of its institution is not yet accomplished. When it is, will revelation testify the fact?

The nature of our subject does not require that any natural feeling be disturbed. The Gospels may be read and studied with increased interest; the bearing of every lesson they contain is simply removed from exterior to interior perception. The Lord Christ did not once live among men; but He is ever living among them, and has so done since the world began. The enunciation made to Mary by the angel Gabriel is sounded in the spirit ears of every woman in existence. All exclusiveness is abolished: every woman is as blessed as Mary. All nations do call her blessed, for by her they obtain re-birth unto righteousness. Had Gabriel descended into the external perception of Mary to enunciate to her the birth of Christ, He must have become a subject of time and space; but, as it was, Mary's spirit opened into that Divine presence in which the angel Gabriel was then, is now standing, and does for ever stand. In that open spiritual condition of natural life did Mary in her inward ear detect and listen to the speech of Gabriel—the messenger of good tidings to men and to women, for he spake of things that should shortly come to pass. Defective mortal consciousness is of no account. But it will be seen that our present purpose is the enlightenment of that consciousness. It is now that light may shine forth in the darkness; it comprehendeth it not; nevertheless, the light shineth. It is not at present possible to cast a brighter light upon revelation; it must do its work, and when that is accomplished, much more will be vouchsafed.

So soon as the life of *interior* nature is attained, all things are made plain; the Scriptures are then unveiled and disrobed of their mysterious clothing. The language in which they are written is conformable to the events it chronicles, one being as mysterious as the other, and both being as distinct in character as can be imagined from the usual course of ordinary human life.

There is no time to the spirit, no hindrance to any mental experience. No tree can attain maturity at once, no fruit ripen in a day; but it is not so in the spirit, for, if the whole tree with its ripened fruit, its seed, its branch and leaf, were not fully developed in its essence, no such creation as a perfect plant could meet the eye of man. It is progressive in his sight—to his perception; but, to the sight of spiritual beings in a high degree of celestiality, progression is unknown: they behold creation, they view the minutest vegetable growing upon the earth—they can do so with a much clearer vision than man is endowed with, but *they do not see the form he sees;* they see perfectly, he imperfectly.

The continuation of these revealings does not depend upon their reception by mankind, for that is tardy in every case of God's dealings with the human mind: the revelation must be made, even though it be received as such by but two or three members of the Lord's Church on earth; that reception is quite sufficient to form a foundation on which to erect a temple, the spire of which shall reach to heaven.

All things hang together by one invisible thread; its vibrations affect the life-springs of every dependant thereon. This work can proceed only as the medium can be admitted into the light; but it is very often necessary to shade her eyes, lest nature be overstrained, and a state induced, which must involve physical dissolution, not from natural, but from interior causes operating upon the corporeal frame in an unusual manner. On this account, it is that much unavoidable hindrance will occur, and patience must be exercised. The influence of the spheres is, at this age, pressing upon every human subject in a manner that has never previously existed, and hence many new and extraordinary events are coming to pass, the object of which is of immense magnitude, but wholly incomprehensible to mankind. The experiences of persons living in past centuries is not of comparable extent to that which will be opened in the present era, and this because the advent of Jesus is now made a mortal comprehension in a manner that has never had previous revelation. "The thoughts of His heart are to all generations." One thought from Him concerning Himself is efficient unto the whole world—for all hold life in Him—live because He lives.

The Lord is in the interiors of nature—that is His advent into nature. He is now in the interiors of every human being, every one being a recipient of natural life. Had He been more present to the disciples of old than He is to us at this day, matters would have deteriorated instead of progressed. God does not vary His attitude in respect of man. He is ever the same; but the life of man is subject to alternations of state. The Lord has revealed Himself in every age in accordance with the ability of man to receive Him. The natural mind is no indication of the interior extent of that reception; if it could interfere to arrest the progress of spirituality in the soul, no flesh could attain unto the heavenly estate. Internal states are altogether independent of the natural senses, and but rarely become a conscious experience. Thus the mind is kept from harm, and the true order of creation inwardly preserved. Mankind are in the hand of God, and not one hair of the head can be touched without His knowledge and permission. Faintness and sickness belong unto nature. Strength and beauty unto the spirit; but, be it remembered, there is a nature clinging to the spirit: nature is not put off by the death of the body, it is *in* as well as *on* the human soul, and it can only be dispensed with by means of *re-birth;* that process has passed upon every *spirit* proper. To the just, it is not a painful experience, save, that tears may fall over memories of past offences committed in the weakness of the flesh. But, courage belongeth unto the righteous, and in all states, the pure in heart see their God. The sin of the just is ofttimes involuntary; it yieldeth its own torment, and the sufferer will be his own physician, cutting out his own canker. With every such removal comes the new-born flesh, till at last the leprosy is healed, and " the flesh of a little child" is upon him.

This is the leprosy of the Scriptures; they treat of spiritual not natural maladies. The Lord healed the spirits of men, but nature made report only of the healing of the body. The Lord lived in the world in the days of leprous Naaman; He healed him as truly as He raised Lazarus. He restored the Syrian's flesh as truly as the withered hand.

To adventure direct contradictions to existing universal opinion is not the wont of mankind; but to spiritual beings it is a high-born privilege; and it is to them a matter of entire indifference as to whether credence or incredulity follow upon their track. Sensuous fallacies are so abundant, that truth can never appear without apparent incongruity.

In Cana of Galilee, the Lord is said to have sat at a marriage feast. There is a spirit sphere within every plot of land the natural foot can tread on; in that sphere moves the Lord of life; in that atmosphere breathes the Lord Jesus. But His footprints are immaterial, His presence imperceptible to the outward eye. The Lord is in the interiors of natural life, consequently, He does truly descend into nature; but He is not, nor ever was a denizen of the world He comes to save. He is so in the *spirit of its life;* therein He hungers and he thirsts; He is weary, and He rests; He sleeps, and is awakened; He weeps, and performs every miracle the Gospels record. He wears the seamless coat; He is scourged and crucified; but not as is supposed; not so in *external* nature; in its *essence,* every event alluded to is as true as truth can be.

These Gospel narratives are enduring unto everlasting life; no wave of time can ever obliterate their stamp on nature; they are *Divine manifestations,* not merely natural ones once occurring on the planes of Palestine. Jesus is, at this day, in the interiors of the land your homes rest on. He is, at this day, sitting at your board, walking at your side, taking your little ones in His arms and blessing them; preaching in the temples of your souls. In the market place, and in the crowded thoroughfare may His divine voice be heard, if the inward ear be kept unstopped; yea, while you hasten on your way to accomplish some mundane matter, Christ and His apostolic band are passing that way too.

There is no age, no time, in which Jesus does not tread in the footprints of humanity. He is with us *now.* He is in us *now.* With some He is receiving birth, with others He is undergoing crucifixion. So with every event; one is not more dependent upon period than another; we each receive Him in accordance with our inward state of reception. With some He walks, with others He sits in a house. With some He dines, with others He sups. Some see Him only passing by, others hold converse with Him in secret. Some are healed by Him in one way, some in another.

The Lord Jesus has descended into nature, into its *interior depths,* into its *essences;* there He has done more "wondrously" than did "the angel of the Lord." He has redeemed humanity, healed the sick, raised the dead, restored the widow's only son, dried the tears of Magdalens, cast out demons, clothed and fed the maniacs; these are a mighty host; not one, or "two men" living among the tombs, "exceeding fierce," but the whole number of "the lost sheep of the house of Israel." These He came to save. He has saved them. But are there no more sick and maimed,—maniacs of the spirit? Is Christ's work accomplished, and does He now rest from His *natural* labours? Believe it not! "He who keepeth Israel neither slumbers nor sleeps." He sleepeth no more in nature than He does in the spirit, He is, at this day, just as present in nature as ever He was in the Gospel age, for of Him no time is predicable. If His Divine manifestation was needed once, it is needed so long as nature exists. To imagine that the Lord *once* was to man what He is not now and for ever, is to pollute the Holy Sanctuary with the grossness of merely sensuous perception; it is not a spiritual idea, but belongs unto the fallacy of natural thought, let it not cumber the fruitful soil of the spirit. The knowledge herewith transmitted to mortals concerning the existence of *interior nature*, will be the means of elevation to their spirits in a degree they cannot, at this present, appreciate. But, lest we should offend one of the "little ones" that believe in Christ, we must not make careless mention of that which they are not yet able to hear; even the strong man must be very carefully fed, and only with morsels at a time.

———

Every man is an Adam and he is a Joseph. Every woman is an Eve and she is a Mary. The Lord is thus present with every human being in the fulness of His divine advent. This enigmatical development of Deity is incomprehensible to the low standard of mortal capacity. The speech of the Lord is also very enigmatical; its object and utility often hard to be surmised. If the mind be not prepared to understand a language that is addressed to it, the effect must be a commixture of incongruous ideas. Sometimes light will appear, and again become obscured, and, finally, no permanent impression will remain. Nevertheless, if the words of that imperfectly understood language are indelibly recorded, subsequent knowledge may make their meaning clear and intelligible. The Gospel scribes wrote that which they did not in the least comprehend; they did so by virtue of a divine influx of which they were receptive.

Peter, James, and John, with other scriptural names, to which may be added "legion," are representative of characteristics and states relative to the spirit of every individual man and woman. This is the mystery of Gospel revelation; regard it no longer as a history of outward nature; it is a divine manifestation of God in nature. God is ever flowing forth in a divine sphere of revelation, but man has not the ear open to hear, nor the eye to see. Let the deaf ears be unstopped, and remove the mortal lens from the eye of the spirit, then will God and revelation be seen in purity and truth.

When Jesus gave up the ghost, and the rocks were rent, how was it that one stone was left upon another in nature at all? Why did not every house fall, *every* man smite upon his breast and say, "Truly this was the Son of God?" No! none but believers heard His voice crying, "Eli, Eli, lama sabachthani;" none but those who had the ear opened to hear the voice that so spake in the recesses of their spirits heard that divine cry, and they that mocked knew not that it was the voice of Deity. They who believe not in the heart inwardly, cannot hear the voice of God outwardly. "He calleth for Elias, let us see if he will come to save Him." Elias was John the Baptist, the natural representative of Christ, the baptizer of water, not of fire. The polluted Jew could only hear the divine voice of God in nature as a purely material manifestation, a dispensation of water.

The lesson to be derived from this portion of my work is twofold; it is both natural and spiritual; it is indicative of the use and object to be obtained by spiritual intercourse, and it is the means by which perplexity of natural belief in divine verities may be removed. If any reader still prefers to consider the advent of Jesus as a material one, he can do so; it will not, in the least, embarrass his onward progress in spiritual advancement: but, if he would have interior truth, it is now placed within his grasp. The more truly we worship Christ, the more closely are we conjoined to His Divine Person, and the more readily can we be admitted into His holy presence. The ground of all spirituality is nature; it must be cultivated, or no seed will germinate in it. The Lord is in this matter as well as in every other, and if you are wise unto salvation, you will attend as circumspectly to the little things of life as to the great ones, for weighty matters rest upon them. The Lord is with the smallest events of life. The circumstance of removal to a new scene, is fraught with important results to the spirits of all who are concerned in it. The recurrence of a past memory is an habitual association of secret thought on that which does not always become a conscious perception, but is ever present to the inward spirit. Thus every moment since you first drew breath is still present to you, it is in you and with you. Such is natural life; spiritual life is similarly constituted, it is likewise an ever-present existence, it is only past to your outward consciousness, to the inward it is the same as when you first came forth of God. This reflection will suffice to shew that time and event are ever present in the Divine mind. We are conceived—live in the womb—are born into nature, pass through every stage of human existence, pass out of time, become spirits,—angels; rise into spheres the mind of man has no conception of; to God it is all one present.

We return to the Gospel narratives. Gabriel foretold of union consummated in the spirit; he told of wars and rumours, he spake of every desolation, of every pang humanity can experience, he gave forth A WORD, he gave utterance to every prophecy. He, Gabriel, opened to the comprehension of mortal woman the whole law and work of creation. He expounded in her spiritual ear the nature of her substance, and divulged the secret springs of her being. All this, and more than language can convey, became to Mary's mind a comprehension and likewise an experience; she then knew how it was with her sisters in the flesh; she knew that *all* were " highly favoured,"—that *every* womb can bear the same burden promised unto her. She pondered these things *in her heart*, as knowing that the world could not receive that which had *opened in her heart*. She gave birth to a divine natural manifestation of the Lord of Life; that is, she was the means of drawing forth into nature such a power of divine life, that a complete renovation of external conditions was the result, and victory over every evil lust became the prerogative of man. Sensuality continued, but it was, by the power of the Highest in the interiors of nature, driven out to the circumference; it was not possible for human beings to be otherwise saved, for they were under the curse of death—death of the spirit—Christ came into that valley of death. He died there; He, the Holy One of God, the Holy natural principle of Deity took upon Himself the curse of fallen humanity, and, in that sphere which is invisible to the sensuous eye, lived and died the Lord Christ Jesus. The Son of God became the Son of Man, He clothed Himself with woman's *interior* natural garment; and it was seamless, whole, and entire, Adamic, as it is in the *inward* life of every woman upon the face of the earth. He was born of her into that nature which every soul enters when it puts off the body of dust; there the righteous assemble with the wicked for the final doom. The babe born of Mary in Bethlehem of Judea *is now* in that region; but it must be reached in the spirit; the spot of terrestrial land so called, is an outbirth of the spirit. If there were not a spiritual region in which you received your spirit birth, no natural space could exist. It is a natural body indicating an imperceptible spirit within.

The fame of Christ's advent into nature was of limited extent; it pervaded the atmosphere, and so Herod heard of Him, and thought His kingdom to be of the earth earthy; but He said, "I am not of this world." Had He dwelt in the world as is supposed, His kingdom and reign *must* have been " of this world," His breath *must* have produced such an effect in and upon all natural substance that it could no longer have retained its adamantine properties. Rocks would have rent asunder, the temple veil have disclosed the holy mysteries within; death would have been vanquished, the tenants of tombs would have walked forth into the holy city, as well at His *birth* as at His death.

The Gospel narratives are personal; they are constructed in the past tense; but to us they are present, and likewise future. Let the word PRESENT be ever indelibly stamped on your minds, and be not oblivious to its meaning. The Lord is at this hour, as present in the fulness of His divine natural advent, as at any hour since the world began. Mary is the interior cognomen of WOMAN : whether she be righteous, or whether she be unrighteous, she cannot be unsexed, therefore, she is formed for giving birth to the Lord Jesus; and, being so formed, give birth to Him she must; she cannot restrain the interior action of her frame, so give birth to Christ she does; and, in the performance of that involuntary act, she effects the redemption of herself and of her masculine counterpart, for, in the sight of God they are *one being*. She is casting the burden of sin upon the Lord's shoulder; she is involuntarily obeying His commands.

A good parent requires his child to perform, or to abstain from the performance of certain acts: but the child is wilful, and acts contrary to the injunctions of the parent. Does he allow it to do so? No;

he *enforces* obedience, and if necessary, inflicts chastisement. He interferes with the disorderly will of the child, and overcomes evil with good. The restraint of the human will is the prerogative of Deity as well as of man, the parental relation being in each case the sanction.

The reality of appearances is very perplexing to the mortal mind; but, after death, the veil is drawn, and natural objects are seen under a very different aspect to that which pertaineth unto corporeal vision. Heat and light are various, in accordance with atmospherical changes, but, in the spirit there is no such change of season. The heart may be more glowing in the winter than in the summer season, and if death then occur, the aspect of *interior* nature will be more genial, than any summer upon earth ever was. If all men were barren of spiritual treasure, it would be always winter; and if all were fruitfully rich, it would be a perpetual summer. The earth is undergoing interior renovation, but outward observation is obscure; it cannot yet become evident, it must first become a matter of faith. Have faith, and then are all things possible with God.

By the view now presented of the Lord's advent, that event is not withdrawn from *natural ultimation;* it is, on the contrary, consolidated upon a rock.

The difference between natural and spiritual thought, is as that of a little child, compared with the meditations of scholastic genius. The Divine Word in its outer form, is for the child-man, but it is regis-

tered in heaven, and is there revealed to angelic
perception. Such is the difference between the
Bible and all other human productions; it contains
light within light, sun within sun, life within life,
culminating in God. It is tempered in its effulgence
to the weakness of every nerve, and its interior
depths are illimitable. Within nature there is a
spirit of natural life, within every natural object on
the earth, there is a living soul; in that sphere, on
that soul, the Lord God Jesus Christ made impress.
The path we are now treading is crowded with every
kind of wayfarer, and all are clamorous for audience.
We cannot find room wherein to place these words,
so manifold are the inquisitorial voices that would
fain be heard; all shall be answered, but not in one
breath, nor on one page. This mystery must be
solved to the comprehension of mankind; they are
gazing on shadows, they have seen the effigy of
Christ on the path of nature, and it has been
elongated to their mental vision, by the setting of
the sun of *interior* nature: that sun is about to rise,
and we shall then behold every object *as it is*, not
only as it *appears*. Natural vision is perfectly distinct from spiritual vision, but, the spiritual objects
that subsist in the interiors of nature, can be drawn
forth into outward nature, and there be seen and
handled just as consciously as any material object.
This is a well known fact to certain individuals who
are not ashamed to bear testimony thereto.

The existence of the Lord Christ in the *interiors*

of natural life, is the personation of God in the flesh; there is no more perfectly natural manifestation that can possibly take place, the life of man being not merely natural as outwardly developed, but likewise so as inwardly constituted. The spirit of nature gives form to the body,—to the mind, with all its concomitants. Christ is, as I have represented Him, a much more truly natural man than He could have been, had He been as is so universally supposed, a man of outward nature only.

It has been stated that the departed babe is no longer such in the spirit spheres to which it is removed by death. A very numerous class of human beings never enter the world of outward nature at all; they die, as it is termed, in the womb, previous to delivery; they do so at every stage of maturation: they pass away, but they are all living entities,—sons of God,—heirs of immortality: they may have manifested natural life in the sanctuary of infants, or they may have been removed previous to that maternal experience; in either case, the life of the germ-soul is entire,—unharmed: they are on that same plane on which Christ makes manifestation of life.

The babe unborn into outward nature, passes from the body of its mother into the *interiors* of nature; there it is not infantile, but a whole undivided Adam, perfect in all respects. The Lord thus passed from Mary's womb; but the Gospel narrates that she took her son and laid Him in a manger, that is, she removed Him from the cognizance of men, and she placed Him where He could only be known to exist by virtue of inward perception. The wise men of the East were supernaturally directed. No man could have pointed out to them the way to find the infant Jesus; for, in the world, He had nowhere to lay His head. These men are figuratively described, they belong to every age and nation. Some men are wise now, and they ever dwell in the East; the morning-star is ever guiding them into the presence of Jesus; they are ever presenting precious inward soul gifts, which are alone acceptable to Him. The Gospel must be preached, and its inner mysteries revealed in the light by which all men receive eastern wisdom. The star by which these wise ones were guided into the divine presence is that light of interior nature which will lead all unto the veritable Christ, as He is to be seen even at this day. The Gospels are not at variance with themselves, neither with any other portion of Scripture. But they are no more to be considered a record of mere earthly transactions than is the severance of Eve from Adam. That circumstance and the birth of Christ into nature, took place upon the same identical plane, and, moreover, if you can hear it, the one event occurred spontaneously with the other, for at this instant Eve severance is going on, and, at this instant, Christ is coming forth of

Mary, and it is in Eden and in Bethlehem of Judea that these events are now occurring. If Eve be woman, Mary is no less so: woman includes both.

The interval of time implied in the Scriptures between these events, does not apply to the spirit, but only to the natural comprehension of mankind, who could in no other way receive the knowledge of such truths. Thus it is that the Bible is so incomprehensible; it is a consecutive account of states through which every human being is at this moment passing, and it is a description of the means provided by God for the restoration of every living soul from the effects of inward declension. These spiritual truths have to be given to ignorant man as he can alone receive them; they cannot be conveyed to his mind in the "twinkling of an eye," or by a stroke of the pen; the idea of time, interval, and epoch, cannot be excluded from his finite perception of spiritual realities, to which time and space have no reference.

To elaborate this theme, we must be allowed both time and space. To construct an edifice that shall supersede that of former ages, we must collect material that could not then be obtained; to fortify it against the attacks of unbelievers in spirit power, we must enlarge upon the well attested facts of the day in which we write. To disregard those things which men of the world call delusions, superstitions, or impositions, would be to commit the sin of Herod; slay all, that the kingdom of the world may be established as the world desires. But, we fear no evil, we know full well that it is there, and that it will come out to defy the armies of the living God; but our stone is smooth, and chosen out of the running brook; it is sure, though it has to slay a giant. "Leave all and follow me." We come—we follow—we pass the boundary of earth—we enter the universe of nature. Following Christ through the womb of woman, we begin our journey with Him from His birth. He entered life a man, as He shewed himself to Adam and to Eve in Edenland; that is, in interior nature. He took upon Himself the cross, ere mankind of Gospel record knew of His existence as man. They knew not that His work of redemption began before they were born; and that He was then putting away the actual sin under which they bent. The Lord was Man past, Man present, and Man for to come. This is Jesus, you and I are with Him now; we are gazing on the various aspects of His divine human countenance, and He is now shewing Himself to us.

Jesus was in nature of spiritual reality not apparent, but *actual human nature* it was that Christ was born into; not born of time, but into time,—not born of space, but into space; manifest in *all time,—all space* since the world began. Was there a time when Jesus was not incarnate? Never since Adam was so. Was there a woman who could not, did not, give Him birth? Never since Eve was. Eve and Mary are not sisters, but they are *one and the same*. There is no individual Eve—no individual Mary. The Gospel narrative applies to humanity; not to a certain number of individuals who surrounded the person of Christ in the flesh.

These things are very trying to the disciples of the Lord Jesus; and many will return and walk no more with us; but we heed it not; our path is straight, and if we have to walk in it alone, we do so. We must here remember that man, whether unitary or in division of race, is still man—Adam. So Christ, whether in one divine person or in many divine persons, is still the same Christ.—One God and one man. The childhood of Christ is that of the race; they have been educated up to the present point,—some have, others have not.—So long as we have children among us, so long must we construct toys for their benefit, and write stories for their edification; but, if there were no children, we should not do thus. We have been God's children; by toy and by story He has instructed us; but now we may put away childish things, and may see Him as MAN, not as a child adapting Himself to our childish necessities. We have led this pen up to the pinnacle of the temple at Jerusalem; but it is Christ who has placed Himself there; for no other power can compete with His; though the appearance be otherwise. The voice is ever crying, "Come unto me all ye that are heavy laden, and I will give you rest." It was never so said once or twice, but ever since mankind needed rest; and that they did long—very long—before Christ is supposed to have uttered these words. No! there is day and there is night, and there is man and there is woman: all is one,—one God, one universe.

There are, at this day, many marvels in process of development; *spiritual manifestations* they are called; these come from interior to exterior nature. Men treat them as they are said to have treated Christ; they believe not in the signs of the times, and cry, "Delusion," and "Imposition;" but men of the spirit know that such things be, yet know not how to explain them, in accordance with scripture and right reason. The truth is, nature is opening her prison-door, and the light of interior nature is shining in upon the people sitting in darkness and in the shadow of death. The revelations of the spirit are manifold,—elevated or debased, but still the selfsame spirit, adapting itself to the reception of man,—man wise, or man simple,—man pure, or man impure. Man thinks there are spirits of every grade and class making manifestation to him; whereas it is all his own spirit, making evident its own interior condition and quality. These facts bear upon our present subject, hence their introduction in this place. Christ is said to have cast out demons who infested the bodies of innocent persons,—children even; but, they are infesting mankind at the present day, they produce all the disease,—all the agony of body and mind that any human being can suffer. Christ, as He has hitherto been seen of men, could only cure "a few sick folk," while the world is teeming with them; they are thronging every thoroughfare in life. Christ, as I have now represented Him, is equal to every emergency, cures every malady, not outwardly, as was supposed, but inwardly; He is born into every clime,—every outlandish savage woman can, and does, give Him natural birth: He can reside in her womb, for she is a Mary, as well as an Eve, and her *internal spiritual* experiences are co-equal. Thus it is that Christ is a universal Redeemer, and divine Sanctifier of the entire range of humanity. The whole of the Scripture from beginning to end must be interpreted according to this rule, for there is not one single exception; and it is in this view *alone*, that the Holy Scriptures can be seen to be the Word of God,—co-eternal and correlative with Him.

The advancing manhood of the race demands this exposition from the pen of the spirit, and in it will be seen the faith of Peter, and the love of John; they are typal men; many are as Peter, and many there are as John: and each disciple may be gathered from among the congregations of the age in which this present writer lives. There are many things yet inexplicable to the natural mind of man in the view I have now given of the Lord Christ, but the main point has been gained, that of removing the plane of vision from *exterior* to *interior* nature. The conception of all abortive births being identical with that of Christ's from Mary, shall be still further dwelt upon, for it must be made clear, otherwise credence will be impossible. The woman called Mary is Eve; she was told that her seed should "bruise the serpent's head," and that she should "bruise his heel;" no one has supposed that the woman to whom this saying is apparently addressed, was to perform this thing, but it has ever been supposed to allude to Mary, as it truly did, but not as an individual. Here then is an evidence that Mary is Eve, and Eve is Mary, and both names are used in scripture language to indicate WOMAN, consequently, in the history of Mary, as well as Eve, we recognize the interior history of every woman in creation.

The Lord is Jesus only in nature,—Christ only in nature; but in His pure divinity He is the Lord God. This is the appellation emphatically bestowed upon Him in the early passages of Scripture history. But we find that the Lord God descended lower and lower in the scale of life; that He accompanied man in every stage of his declension; making manifestation of presence in proportion to man's capacity of reception. When He could no longer be received as the Lord God, He came as the Lord-Man. He made to man the natural demonstration he needed; Christ in nature adapted Himself to the reception of every capacity. Jesus came to work upon the spirits of mankind, not merely to heal their bodies, but by manifesting Himself to their spirits spiritually, He affected their bodies naturally; He also produced an effect upon the natural mental development, such as no other dispensation was adequate to accomplish. He rent a veil that shall never again obscure the vision of humanity. The Lord came into nature so soon as the need for that advent occurred,—it did so when Adam left the paradise of his first blessed estate.

To every man there is a Genesis, and likewise a Gospel; that is, the birth of Christ into nature. The Lord is incarnated in every woman, otherwise she could not be woman, Mary as well as Eve,— every woman is as much one as the other. Every man is as much Joseph as Adam, and there is no separation possible,—Adam and Joseph are the same: neither are individuals in an *exclusive* sense. The same is applicable to every human being: the Lord is not born of one more than another. The birth— incarnation of Christ in the person of woman—is just as essential to the maintenance of her spiritual and natural life as is the severance of Eve from the person of Adam; and, it is just as universal. For this purpose was the severance effected; not merely to bring forth children, but to give birth to the Lord Christ in that nature to which man and woman descended; for He is the seed of the woman bruising the serpent's head. Did He not do this in and for every Adam and every Eve, they could not accomplish the work of salvation in themselves. But, the Lord does it for them by allowing Himself to be born into their nature. In that material nature He appears as a babe, but to the spirit in the spirit He is ever the Lord Christ, preaching and working miracles, casting out devils, and raising the dead.

The Lord is thus incarnated in woman by virtue of her *inward* conjunction with man; if she be externally married, she still incarnates the Lord Jesus: but not by virtue of that outward connection: the husband may be her true partner or not; in either case, the conception of the Saviour of her soul will be *wholly spiritual*,—it is the conception of Mary,—the overshadowing of the Power of the Highest; and the spirit will be alone conscious of experiences that belong unto itself.

Prophecy does but assert fact. It was the betrayal of woman's secret nature that the ancient seers disclosed; they were truly prophets, for they wrote of that which God alone revealed to them concerning the birth of Jesus into nature. That was the mission of the inspired Isaiah; he wrote of that which had been since the world began; but he knew not from nature that such things could be; he was elevated into regions wherein he heard and saw that which fell into the natural language he has used; that is prophecy. Mankind are progressive; they may now, if they will, see, as no man hath seen heretofore; and, if they will, they may now hear that which hath not heretofore fallen upon the mortal ear. The Lord is in their midst, there is no home where He is not—there is no woman who has Him not as her son, her Lord and her God. There is no man who has not, *in the spirit*, contributed to His birth into nature; but in the part performed by man and that by woman there is difference; on this account, Mary is several times presented to the view of the gospel reader, whereas Joseph is soon lost sight of. Woman has, through life, a much more natural part to perform than man, hence her personal attendance upon the Lord as narrated in the Gospels.

It is not for any disputation to meet us at this point. Testimony is herein given to the establishment of an heretofore unrevealed verity; but if comprehension fail, we refer to the Lord Christ, who is present in the soul and in the body of every member of His Church on earth, as well as above it. The inward mind of man does always dwell in the presence of Deity, independently of His manifestation in the flesh of nature. Nature comprehends two worlds, one spiritual the other natural: the mind is ever active upon both.

The Evangelists are found to vary in the details of the Gospel records, simply because they each followed a distinctive impulse. They knew not wherefore or of what they wrote any more than does the scribe of these present writings, know how her pen writes of such unheard-of things; nature does not know of that which passes in the spirit; it is only conscious of effects, not of interior causes. The Word of God was thus written word by word; no inspired penman knew anything about what he was doing, nor why he thus acted; but he was impelled by a divine voice within, and it was the voice of Christ that thus dictated His Word to humanity. It was Himself writing of Himself; and it is a divine record that is thus compiled; it is no part of it traditional, but is given by immediate inspiration from God.

It is not seemly for us herein to enter into argument, or to adapt our speech to earthly criticism or disquisition; it pertaineth not unto the spirit of this natural act so to do; but it is permitted in the councils of Providence that an answer should be granted to the extent of human capacity to receive. The Lord is as nigh of hearing now as if He were on earth. He is ever in the earth, though He never was, nor ever will be, on its surface. Mankind have, in the Gospels, seen His shadow passing by; they may now see His person; they may take Him into their homes, and He will give them of His body and of his blood. His Divine Body is that human principle which mankind receive from Him pure and undefiled,—it has become defiled, so He incarnates Himself, purifies, renovates it, and then says unto all men, "Take eat,"—appropriate—"this is my body,"—"This is my blood, that of the new covenant which is shed for many,"—He that eateth Me liveth by Me." These words apply to natural life, of which eating can alone be predicated. In this form, the inspired Evangelist clothed a great internal verity. He wrote of things that were shortly coming to pass,—of that which was then passing,—and of that which had been from "the beginning." When Jesus walked, as it is expressed, in the garden, and called unto Adam and Eve, saying, "Where art thou?" It was just as essential *then* that man should eat the Lord's body in order to have life in Him, as ever it was.

The natural conception has constructed the narrative,—clothed the spiritual reality with that body in which it appears on earth. But, it is so done in strict accordance with the Divine Will, and perfectly accomplishes the divine purpose in its construction. It heals the sick, unstops deaf ears, opens blind eyes, casts out devils, raises the dead, bears divine power into nature. It will continue its work of salvation. Instruction is thus afforded to the simple and child-like mind. Christ is beloved—worshipped—trusted. Prayer is offered to Him. His example is followed, —at least the effort is made. But to the strong man of the spirit meat is now presented; take it, if it is homogeneous to your requirements, and if it is not, live still on the babes' milk, for it is holy nutriment, despise it not. If it were to cease flowing, no flesh could sustain life either in spirit or in nature, for one life is dependent upon the other.

The Lord is ever with man; he may turn aside from the path of rectitude, but the Lord follows him into that path. The Lord is angry with the wicked every day; consequently He careth for the wicked. If He cared not for them, He could not be said to be angry with them. But anger in God is not exemplified by anger in man. Man is every day angry with his fellow, and it implies dislike and desire to punish. But in God anger implies *love* and desire to draw man to Himself. God is jealous; but not as that passion is exhibited in man. God is desirous that man should fall down and worship before Him; but, He desires it not as man delights to receive homage from his fellow man. God loves all alike. Man does not, and can not love all alike; in man such universality of affection would be indicative of disorder. Thus we see that God is not adequately represented by any human being; and yet the good are well able to appreciate the attributes of Deity, and to love and worship accordingly.

The Lord is appreciated in the degree and to the extent that He shews Himself to man. In the estimation of one, He is a God of love; and in the estimation of another, He is a God of wrath,—one who is angry with the wicked every day. He is of both attributes; but his belongings are to usward. What God is in and to Himself may no man essay to know. He is God, and He doeth what seemeth Him good with His own. But His own can only know Him as He is pleased to shew Himself unto them. He left His high estate and came down to His own, but they did not then know Him, and, consequently, received Him not. Had the Lord manifested Himself to His own as they *knew* Him, they would have received Him with joy; but He did not desire to be thus received of them. The Lord came as He desired to be received. His advent was not a failure. Ere He condescended to walk with men, the course of His holy footprints were traced; any deviation from which would have disarranged the entire plan of redemption. Had evil not existed, no man would have needed redeeming; but, in consequence of every man and every woman having to be "born again," the Lord comes to every one according to the individual need. The good are born again as well as the bad: Nicodemus has to be reborn; then he will not fear to visit the Lord in light as well as in darkness. Mary, who gives Him birth, must herself be born again. The Lord must be born as each one can receive Him. The Lord is born not for Himself, but for us. He is so born because we, one and all, require re-birth. If we were good we should not require it; we do so because we are evil. All humanity is evil,—all is under the curse of sin, of disobedience. If it were only one man, or one woman who had strayed from the right path, the Lord must be born for them,—He must take into Himself their nature, in order to redeem it from that sin. He, the Lord God, is so born for every child that opens the matrix. But, there are children of every class and grade of evil coming into natural life with every breath the heaving bosom of humanity can draw. These have each one a separate consciousness, a separate identity, and require a separate personal redemption. They have it; they are one and all saved,—redeemed from death of evil to life unto righteousness; not by any one redemption epoch effected by our Lord in the flesh. "He saved others, Himself He cannot save." Such would be the cry of lost humanity, if *any soul* were to escape salvation at the hands of the Redeemer,—Christ. But the Lord has saved and does save Himself. His body is humanity,—His life in nature, the life of humanity, He is Man. He, the Lord-Christ, was not *once* Man, but He was *ever* Man, and He *is still* Man; and so long as man can appear upon this earth, so long will Christ be Man dwelling in the essence of humanity.

The Gospels are descriptive events said to have occurred when Christ was a man in nature. These things are as spiritual as the severance of Eve from Adam in the garden of Eden. No man witnessed *that* transaction; neither did any man witness the advent of Christ into nature; for, one event as well as the other, occurred upon the plane of life we term *interior nature*. There it was the breach occurred, and consequently, there it could alone be repaired. This truth has not as yet reached the perceptions of mankind, but they need not fear; they are not yet aware of the "many things" which Jesus has yet to reveal unto them, and He waiteth only the opening of receptive faculties. He is daily coming to His own, but they receive Him not. They read not the face of the times, and wonder how such things can be. To His chosen band of disciples, the Lord is ever revealing Himself as He is not known of the world. Believe then that His kingdom is not of this world, but yet it is *in* the world; it is a kingdom of spirit—of *inward*, not of *outward* nature.

In the glass of nature is reflected every object existing in nature, but the objects seen in that glass are not the objects themselves, but merely the reflection of them. Christ came in *reality*, not by reflection merely; He was as much the Redeemer of one as of another; He cast not out one devil leaving another in possession; He left no bier untouched by His divine human hand; no issue of blood unstaunched; no eye unopened; no ear unstopped; no impotent man uncured; no Magdalen unforgiven. To *every* soul diseased—imperfectly developed—came He the Lord Jesus. To every defiled sinner is He present; and *every* devil is, to this day, crying out to Him, "Torment me not, I know thee who thou art,"—the Holy one of God. Reality—truth stereotyped by every human breath since nature had birth from God, is herein made manifest. Period and epoch does not apply to scriptural revelation. God is—truth is. Man sins with one breath, is redeemed with the next. The work is ever going on; redemption is now, this is the day of Christ's birth into nature, and this is the day of His crucifixion, and every stage of His progress—every event, every miracle is *now*—at this hour in process of natural operation; the Gospels contain the record of it; they are as prophetic, as historical; they chronicle the mental history of the human mind; they portray its necessities, and describe how those necessities were met and supplied by the advent of the Lord Christ into nature. So soon as man needed a Saviour, came Christ and walked in the garden of his inner nature. He took upon Him man's debased estate, and redeemed every sin that man had or could commit. But it needeth not that God should provide for casualties, for He is ever present: so He meets them all as they occur, He taketh up the broken thread, and the garment is made whole.

John is said to have laid his head on the Lord's breast when he sat with Him at the Last Supper; but in the record ascribed to him, all allusion to this Last Supper is omitted. John is at this day resting his head on the Lord's breast at supper. The Evangelist wrote, not knowing of what, any more than it is said Peter knew of what he spake, when on the mount of transfiguration he proposed to erect three tabernacles, one for Jesus, one for Moses, and one for Elias.

The Scripture writers were one and all spiritual

writers. The present scribe is also a spiritual writer; but the Scriptures are holy inspired documents, to be piously venerated in all ages by all classes of men. This book is not then on a par with any of the Sacred Scriptures. They are prophetic, which this is not; they are written in mysterious language, symbolical, nothing of which applies to this book; it is explanatory of the Scriptures, admitting of no comparison with them. It is the age which differs. The scriptural age was prophetic, the present age is the fulfilment of prophecy. In a future age, the world will receive by the same means, that of involuntary writing, such a measure of holy revelation as it could, at this present, by no means take into its bosom. The human brain will not yet contain the knowledges that are in store for future generations. No comparison can possibly be instituted between the writings of one age and those of another.

The purpose of every revelation is elevation of the human mind to the highest point to which it is accessible. The Lord is thus giving Himself birth in us. He is thus dwelling among us. In all states He is present; to every order of mind He makes Himself comprehensible; to some He is more comprehensible in the spiritual degree, to others in the natural degree; but in the celestial or highest degree of human reception, He has not, hitherto, revealed Himself to any. In this book, He is revealed as never at any previous period; yet, this is very inefficient to portray Him as He is in Himself, or in His relation to mankind. The Lord is Human, hence we are so; He is man, hence we are men; He is woman, hence we are women.

The Lord Christ took upon Himself our nature, but we first obtained it from Him. He is our prototype. Christ is the first man; that is, He was man before all time. He was man dwelling with the Father in that glory which He had before the world was. Christ and the Father are one; there is no division of attributes, consequently, none of parts. Substance is in reality indivisible. It is time and space which cause apparent division; but these are natural perceptions which have no part in God. Time and space are wholly referable to nature not to interior but exclusively to the outward body of nature —to the mere earthlife. These obstacles to true spiritual perception of divine verity are not to be unadvisedly removed; they are earthen pillars on which the heavens rest.

The Lord is described to us as entering life an infant, growing in strength and in stature, increasing in favor with God and man. The Lord does so grow and increase in favor with every man, as he, man, merges from infancy to manhood. To our little children He is not known as the God of our manhood. The simple in heart and in wisdom are seeing Him, portraying Him to their mental vision as He truly is to them. They love to dwell upon His words and to contemplate His acts as performed upon the earth of present abode. These are the Lord's earthly

K

disciples; they follow Him in the divine life; but the believing centurion would rather that Jesus came not into his house, for he feels that he is not worthy; having offices to perform in nature that are not compatible with the divine presence in that same natural degree. The elevated mind of the centurion knows that the personal natural presence of the Lord Christ is not essential to the restoration of his servant to health. We are enunciating the centurion's doctrine. Joseph of Arimathæa, was a devoted disciple of Jesus, yet he followed Him not through the streets and byways of earth. Nicodemus and many others believed, but followed not His earthly footsteps; neither received they Him into their habitations. No! these loved the Lord, and inwardly renewed their daily strength in Him; but they desired not His earthly presence; they intercepted his progress to their natural homes, feeling that His spiritual internal presence was all-sufficient unto salvation.

But that light and knowledge may abound, we will meet the natural mind on its own plane. The Gospels are not literal facts as narrated, Joseph of Arimathæa, is a Gospel character, that is, a typal one; there are, at the present day, not many of his stamp; there are Peters and there are Johns, and every disciple following the Lord, may be, at the present day, clearly identified throughout Christendom, but not the discerning centurion, nor the just Arimathæa. These are prophetic representatives of a church about to be established upon the earth; and the future revealings to be made to that church will cast a light of divinity over the Gospel records in which they have never yet shone.

Inspiration is a natural effect produced by unknown and interior spiritual action. This pen is, in that sense, inspired, but it is not on that account infallible, it may be at any moment turned aside from the path of truth; whether it be so or not, is for every reader of this writing to make his own observation, and to draw his own conclusion; for it is held in a fallible,—natural hand. The Gospel writers were all men of integrity, possessing various mental capacities and diverse natural temperaments; but they each one submitted to the inward dictate: they believed they were recording a natural history, and could believe no otherwise. Luke affirms that he thought it good to follow the example of others, in that he should also write a gospel, "having had perfect understanding of these things from the very first." Truly, Luke had understanding thereof, but not from any *natural* instruction, for he took his own course, not framing his gospel after the preceding ones, nor producing it in accord with that which follows; He had *inward* understanding of that *spirit gospel* which he was to embody in nature's language. If the Lord will be revealed by the mouth of His holy prophets; the Scriptures are their speech. The Lord is from everlasting to everlasting, and to place His advent in one age more than in another, is to set bounds to the divine manifestation of His power to save His people from their sins.

The Lord is represented as appearing in public only three years of His life in the world; but that is sufficient to indicate, that His mission did not depend upon times and seasons: for, what was He about in the interim, between His temple demonstration and His baptism in Jordan? His "Father's business" was then in process of transaction, just as much so before as after it; but no man had the commission to write of Him during that interval, in which He is said to have been subject unto Joseph and Mary. The Lord was then so interiorly at work with man, that no natural record could be given of His words or of His actions; had He been, as is supposed, a young man growing up *naturally* "in wisdom and in stature, and in favor with God and man," some reliable scribe would most certainly have thought it good to set down something concerning Him. But, on this head, even received tradition remains silent; no human voice may sound forth any rumour of those days. Christ in the world, and no mention made of Him! Where were the Eastern magi, that they sought Him not again? where were the temple rabbis, that they enquired not for the superhuman boy, who had so amazed them by His mysterious converse? These sought Him not, for He had fulfilled His mission unto them, and they desired Him not again. His work was not in any human flesh put upon His divine spirit. He came in the Ethiopian's skin as well as in that of the fair European; every grade,—every particle of human flesh that has ever,—can ever exist, is *in* Him,—*on* Him,—abideth in Him, if it have life; otherwise it can have none.

Mystical interpretation will not serve us here. The existing church is very mystical: nature is spiritualized, literal interpretation abolished. We come to restore *the letter*, to stamp it in nature, to materialize the Gospels, to give life to that body which ignorant man has crucified. We shew forth the *risen* Christ, the *ever-present* God, whom no man can exclude.

The mystery attaching to the youth and early manhood of the Lord Jesus, is to be briefly explained; but it is of difficult comprehension to unspiritual minds: and therefore, if any fail to derive edification therefrom, it must remain to them an unsolved problem. I will not slack my speech till every admissible explanation be afforded to mortals; but, I have no power to enlighten understandings, or to compel belief, neither is it essential that all men should give heed to our speech. Those to whom it is bread, will not be slow to take and eat, perceiving that it is the Lord's body.

The Lord is born in us,—is living,—is crucified,—is laid in the sepulchre by us,—is risen in us,—is entering the upper chamber where we are sitting with closed doors which are found to be no obstacle to His entrance among us. Thomas doubted, therefore the Lord is shewing him His hands and His pierced side. He is referring all men to His *natural history*, and says, "It is I myself," and the incredulous disciple is crying out, "My Lord and my God." "Behold I am with you always, even unto the end of the world;" that is, not after a mystical manner, but as He was when the words of the record fell on the ear of nature, and were impressed upon the soul. That was the voice of Jesus, giving utterance to His own Gospel,—speaking to us through His servants the Evangelists, as He had formerly done through His holy prophets. All heard His divine voice dictating to them the words they should write down; and after such wise, was the Gospel written. Jesus is its author; He did Himself, by His divine advent in the flesh, give human articulation to the Gospel words,—did tell of all that is therein recorded of His marvellous acts, and of His divine speech, of which none had previously any knowledge; for it pertained to the kingdom of nature, only as referable to nature. His *inward* action and influence upon humanity took to itself that body; otherwise it could not be seen or revealed to the natural capacity, which must be met in its weakness, and tenderly ministered unto by the Divine Hand.

There is now no need to reject the Gospel narrative as untrue; it is much more true than is yet supposed; for every incident is pregnant with a meaning, the interpretation of which would—so to speak—go nigh to fill the world with books, if all were to be written. But we speak with the tongue of infancy; language faileth us. The Lord is in the Gospels, not only in the spirit, but in the very language employed by the Evangelists; all of which was, as I have said, dictated to them by the voice of God manifest in the flesh of nature. Thus, I affirm, the Lord's words are not merely reported by the writers, be they inspired or not, but the narrations are given in the Lord's *own* words, none other being used.

The Lord gave forth the Decalogue, and likewise the Gospels, word by word into the human ear; and by so doing, the facts recorded are made *divine*, not merely natural facts. The period of the Lord's retirement in the house of Joseph and Mary, is not to be lightly passed over, for it was the most important epoch of His advent; it was *then* that He performed every miracle,—spake every word, that is subsequently related of Him: hence the Gospels are compiled in the *past* not in the present tense. The Lord acts upon us in *secret*, and we perceive not His divine presence in our souls, and in our bodies; we are not *conscious* that we live by Him, and hold our life in Him: that is the period of His growth in "wisdom and in stature, and in favor with God and man." He does so as well after as before the temple manifestation of Godlike wisdom. He groweth up in us, but we are ignorant of His divine presence; He becometh manifest, and He relateth to us all that has *secretly* been accomplished within us. This is Jesus of Nazareth,—God and man, whom no man can know, save the Father draw him. He was born in Bethlehem of Judæa, located in Jerusalem, was heard and seen on the shores of Galilee, and was beloved in Bethany. These terrestrial planes were the exponents of inward *mental* regions, on which the Christ-foot is *ever* planted.

A divine power is inherent in all that the human hand is set upon; the manifestation of it is in the conception. Man has no ability independent of God; but in operation, much fallibility and weakness is apparent. The Lord has been drawn forth into nature by the effect of the declension and fall of man from the primitive order of his life. The Lord is therefore manifest to us in weakness, in sorrow, and in temptation. He is shewn to us as " a man of sorrows and acquainted with grief." But wherefore? The Scripture answers: "The Lord hath laid upon Him the iniquity of us all." He bears our sins and carries our burdens; He is therefore "afflicted and heavy laden." Could any burden be heavy for the Lord to bear? Had He the universe upon His shoulder, would it oppress Him? Wherefore did He weep and groan, sweat and pray? Was it for Himself, or was it for us that He did so? It was never so done for Himself. Christ was, is, both God and Man. The manifestation of Divinity is in Jesus, likewise the manifestation of Humanity, distinct yet united. He who had the hosts of heaven at His control, yet followed the band of soldiers sent to take Him. This narration is not a mortal fact. Jesus allows Himself to be thus taken in every human being; in whom, and with whom, every event the Gospels record is *daily* taking place. The crucifixion is essential to the salvation of every living soul ; therefore it is past through in the interiors of every living soul. The well disposed are not exempt from the sin of Christ's crucifixion; *they* must live by it as well as the ill-disposed. But the part performed by either class is different. The good man does not know the Lord as He is,—does not recognize His flesh advent in the only true and universal sense; hence he is sacrificing the Lord of life, is giving Him over unto persecutors and blasphemers. But not so with any degree of responsibility. He is washing his hands from " the blood of that just man." Like unto Pilate's wife, the inner consciousness affirms the fact of injustice having been committed on the person of Christ. The evil man is reviling Him, is active in the deed of crucifixion; for *both* Christ is daily dying, is likewise daily rising, is daily being born of woman. The crucifixion is the crowning point of the redemption, which the Lord comes into us in order to effect. The Lord must die as He is *outwardly* apprehended, that He may live as He is *inwardly* apprehended.

These ideas are not new ; they are so to the outward thought alone. I draw them down into nature, clothing them with a natural body such as they can alone at present wear. The Lord is not known in *fulness* by any human being. He is equal to any emergency that may transpire in future ages of the world. He can shew Himself to us; then we know Him; of whom then is God known as He is? He is so known of *every man in existence;* but not in natural consciousness. Spiritual consciousness is to natural as different as light from darkness; the one has no affinity with the other, and yet one is dependent upon the other,—one cannot be without the other, for by the one we define the other. So it is that the Lord would be known of man in nature, that light may thereby abound, and though He be crucified of all; that very act is the cause of His ascension from the sepulchre; without crucifixion, there can be no ascension. Is it then desirable to imbibe falsity that truth may abound? Nay! but seeing error is rampant, it is met by ascendant truth. Had man never fallen, Christ had not been born in the soul: should we not then have known Him? More truly than is possible from the fact of His being born in us: we should then have known Him *as He is;* we now know Him only as He is conceived in us. We are all unfallen in the *inmost* of our spirits: and *there* it is that we know the Lord in truth, and in fulness. There are seasons when this inner mental perception is opened, even into the outer consciousness; but it closes up its portals when the day of the outer world begins to break. In sleep the spirit is awake, and returns to God who gave it; it is then fed by Him and returns to earth laden with the bread of heaven. On no other condition could any soul retain spiritual life; it must sleep in nature that it may be awake in the spirit; it alternates, passing from earth to heaven, and from heaven to earth; the world is obtuse, and will not credit this statement; it sleeps, and finds it true.

The Lord is known as He is to every human being; but not so in natural consciousness, that makes report of Him in accordance with the Gospel narratives; but in the consciousness of the spirit, these histories are unknown; yet our immortal souls are fed, sustained in life by these very histories. The mind must dwell upon the advent of Christ into nature, as being essential to the salvation of souls; this forms the foundation of every conception the human mind is capable of. This is the object to be attained by the inspired pages; they form the basis of the heavens; they must be implanted in the mind as containing divine truth; but men can only receive it in a natural, not in a divine garb.

The truth has now been presented under a different aspect to that it has appeared in since the world began; but I have not yet shewn it forth in every point in which it is accessible to man. The Lord does not appear the same to one that He does to another; for, as human nature is diverse, though constituting one whole; so does the Lord manifest

Himself in all, to all, by being born of each according to the nature of the individual flesh he comes to redeem. If we should be enabled to convey our impression of the divine Saviour to the mind of another, it would be as distinctive from his own conception of Him, as are the characteristics which distinguish men from one another; and yet one idea might be as true as the other. Natural perception is always diverse—spiritual perception is so too; but inward celestial perception is unvarying, uniform. Hence it is that Christ cannot be all in all to all men, unless He be born of each one as He can be alone received. But the Gospels represent Him under one and the same aspect, that is, as a natural man with divine qualifications. They are so written that each one may take Christ into his heart as he can best receive Him, and the effect upon the *inner* consciousness will be perfectly conformable in every human spirit.

Christ Jesus is the Lord God who erst appeared to Adam and to Eve; who made manifestation of divine presence in every phase of appearance recorded from Genesis to Revelations. In each of the several modes of His adaptation to human infirmity, He is the Lord God—Omnipotent, Omnipresent. Jesus then is not less so now than He was in the Gospel age. How should He, seeing He changeth not, and is with us still, "even unto the end of the world?" Jesus is with us, and has so been from the period of His advent in Eden. But He is seen with very different eyes when we read the Old Testament to those we view Him with when we read the New. He is the same Lord, but man regards Him in a different aspect at one age to that of another. Man is of progressive development; therefore the Scripture accompanies him in progression. The Holy Scriptures are written for the benefit of man; they meet his low estate, they are in themselves undefiled verity; they contain germs of unrevealed truth; germ folded within germ—seed within seed—life within life. They record the history of angels as well as that of men; they treat of the kingdom of spirit as well as that of nature; they are established in the heavens as well as upon the earth. These records are supernatural, and all that is so is accommodational to the fallen condition of humanity. Mankind are fast growing out of the childish estate which they inherited from debased Adam; they are becoming *men*. The God-image within is growing forth into nature, and it will not abide in the former palace; former things are passing away; and all things must be made new. New heavens and a new earth must be established: "Behold, I make all things new." The Lord is doing this; He is restoring the old foundations; He is building up the city; it is not new to Him, but to us it is very new; it is so simply because we did not know of its previous existence.

Thus the Lord Christ was from everlasting, but no man knew Him till He revealed Himself by means of the holy Gospels. He is only known as it pleaseth Him to reveal Himself; and He has shewn us that all revelation is progressive; it descendeth to earth only as it can be received; and the measure is pressed down in accordance with its dimension. But it is filled from the same floor, and the grape is pressed from the same vintage. So much as man can receive so much is given into his bosom. But the Gospels are vessels holding wine as well as water, they are by Christ appointed for the renovation of the spirit, as for purification of the body, and they contain wine which He distils from the grape of His own vine. The Lord made man receptive of Himself with every age of his existence. The Lord accommodates His presence to the faculty of man to sustain it. He shews Himself to childhood and to manhood. He is in the world in a manger, yet "the heaven of heavens will not contain Him." He takes upon Himself the nature of man—enters the womb of woman, but He regardeth not one more than another; one is not "highly favored" over another,—one cannot be "the mother of my Lord" to the exclusion of another. It is WOMAN who can be mother to the Lord in His natural advent. She is not more blessed in one guise than in another, for salvation belongeth unto one as to another; and the Lord is a universal parent. He regardeth not the life of one more than another; He has made all alike. Therefore "Mary" is "woman" in the like sense that Eve is woman; and the Lord of life regardeth the whole human race in one collective form as MAN and WOMAN.

The Lord God does not distinguish individuals from among their fellows. He looketh upon man. He will be born of His feminine part in *inward* union with *outward* severance: that portion of man's soul is called, in Scripture language, "Mary." In Bethlehem of Judea He will be born of her: that locality indicates the natural portion of her consciousness, which can alone receive Him. Nature is the body of spirit. Natural space portrays mental development: it is not stationary, but is entirely dependent upon state. A space of land may be covered with habitations, or it may be void. Space is then subject to mental cultivation, and adaptation to the necessities of mankind. Thus Bethlehem is to be considered as the garden of Eden; non-existent so soon as Adam and Eve leave it; but for other Adams and Eves it is hourly coming into experience. "So be it unto me," is said by every woman. As Eve spake to the Lord, saying, "The serpent beguiled me, and I did eat;" so does woman in the spirit give utterance to her inward sin, and confess her need of a Saviour from that sin.

It is very good that we should hold the letter of the divine Word in veneration; and, when we have seen in what it consists, we shall esteem it of infinite, instead of merely finite importance; we shall then see that it is *truly* "settled in heaven;" that its magnitude is beyond all mortal estimation. Moreover, we shall then be enabled to comprehend the saying, that, if all the acts of God in the flesh were to be enumerated, the whole world would not contain the books that should be written. Of these things knoweth no man; but they may be known. Jesus does not act for one generation only, but for generations yet unborn.

When mankind can look on Jesus, as He is now transfigured before them, without fear, then will the cloud no longer envelope Him,—obscuring their natural vision. But on mountain heights the atmosphere is rarified, and does not suit the lungs of humanity; they cannot draw their breath,—sustain their mortal life with the same vigor that they do on the plains. The disciples tremble, and are "sore afraid;" but they are men, and they are babes; they require both meat and milk: they must be nourished by both; and milk—the babes' food—developes the man. When Jesus is taken away as man, then they are not afraid to meet persecution, stripes and death: but when He is with them—present to the eye of nature, they are troubled, confounded, and flee from Him as sheep having no shepherd. Mankind are dismayed at the report that Jesus is not to be considered a man of nature, born into the world of one Mary of Bethlehem: but it is only a temporary fear; they may flee apace, but soon Peter will return and warm himself in the court of the High Priest's house. He will not confess the Christ, but his speech betrayeth him; he is a Galilean; he has followed Christ in the nature he formerly beheld Him in; so his interior senses can be opened to the voice of inspiration,—revealing Jesus as the believing disciple did not previously recognize Him.

The Lord not being born of any one woman, He could not be manifest in nature external, but must be so only to the interior perception of mankind. He did not desire to make an external, but solely an internal impression upon them. Had the Lord come forth into the outer world, an impression would have been made upon the natural senses of those who associated with Him, that could never have been subsequently obliterated; the memory of His acts and sayings would have been so indelibly impressed upon their hearts and minds, that no spiritual impression concerning them could have gained any ascendancy over their spirits; men would have conceived that His advent related to the body only, and His mission would have been utterly frustrated.

The Lord Jesus is a Saviour from spiritual wickedness in high places: He is also a present Saviour; He does not act once for all, but He acteth ever, and is never weary of His work,—the salvation of the race. The Lord is ever with his people, and He is the same yesterday, to-day, and for ever. If He had been once upon a time in the world more naturally than He is so at this our day, He could, in no sense, be understood to be the same now as then. His Divine Human Personality must have been more natural,—more cognizable to mortal sense at one period than at another. The Lord would have degraded Himself, without elevating us;—naturalized His Divine Person, without spiritualizing ours: but, He has allowed us to form perfectly natural conceptions concerning His advent in the flesh; He has Himself, by means of the inspired Evangelists, led us into a perfectly natural path, whereon His footprints can be very legibly traced. It is so done in order that we may follow Him by combining nature and spirit together,—that the dust of earth may be used, whereby our blind eyes may be opened. This is the meaning of the Lord's spittle being mixed with earth, forming clay. The Lord desires that natural sense should be ministered unto, natural requirement supplied, natural feeling enlisted; therefore, He causes Himself to be naturally manifested to us, but, in such wise, as that we may view Him in the mist, and with the halo of distance enveloping His Holy Person. He desires that mystery and ambiguity may accompany every conception of Him as God in the flesh. It has ever been thus: the records are not given by eye-witnesses, but were written many years after the advent was supposed to have taken place; shewing that Christ must, as a natural man, ever be contemplated from under the veil of obscurity.

The Lord is thus naturally as well as spiritually apprehended. He is now rising from the sepulchre, and He is shewing Himself to us as we have never before seen Him. Still He is not resplendent as He may, to a future age, appear. He is yet mystical. We love Him, worship Him; but, if we examine ourselves, we shall find that we cannot with truth affirm that we yet fully understand either Himself or His mighty works, which are wrought in our souls. This deficiency is but the natural infirmity of mankind; it is the body which Christ takes wherewith to clothe His divine Human principle, and in it we behold our Lord and our God. This is His infirm Humanity; His sufferings and death are ours; His crucifixion is the death of the wicked, that which they undergo in their hell, that of interior nature. That the Lord should effect salvation merely by living on the earth, and dying on its surface, is a heresy only applicable to the dark ages that are fast rolling away:—mists of error and false conception which good men have vainly tried to concentrate into a luminary, wherewith to guide their fellows to the Throne of God most High. It is no eastern star, and they who would be wise in the spirit will follow it no more.

We have said that which has not heretofore been whispered into any mortal ear. We have divulged that which was not cognizable to any mortal sense; and we have thereby surprised and perhaps confounded even the wisdom of the just. The Lord has thus far told us some of the many things concerning His advent into nature. He has upheld us so far; but we need to be much more strengthened in the things that belong unto the spirit. We have not yet seen the Lord as He is, but only as He has shewn Himself to men. The Lord is independent of all time; season and epoch do not pertain to the advent of His spiritual presence in and with mankind. The Lord was born of woman, that is, He partook of her substance; He took to Himself a body from her body. That frame He made divine, glorified, resuscitated. He did not put it off, but He glorified that frame which He inherited from His mother Mary. The truth is, that He took only such portion of her body as *could* be glorified, touching not the earthborn particles, but taking into Himself the *spirit* particles, such as pertain only to the life of *interior* nature. He took of that body in which woman inherits eternal life; but in the life of interior nature it is just as natural as that which sustains life upon the *surface* of nature. The Lord Jesus was born as a child of that *interior* natural body; and in that frame He made manifest His divine presence in nature. But He was not more present in the land of Palestine than He was at the antipodes. He was no more naturally present in one age of mortal life than He is at another; and if we would *truly* see the Lord Jesus *as He is*, and as He *now* desires to shew Himself to us, we shall behold Him in the interiors of our mortal senses; we shall recognize His Divine

Presence in our souls, and in our bodies also; for He is in our thoughts as a Divine human personality, and He has so enabled us to receive Him by virtue of the Gospel narrative. By no other means could any being have received Him as the Lord Christ; by no other means could the knowledge of, and faith in, the Divine Incarnation and human redemption thence effected, have reached the natural perceptions of mankind. Therefore the Gospels are a most holy record of *facts*,—of *means* by which the human race are saved—rescued from eternal condemnation and death. They are a distinct revelation to man of the power of the Highest to cause His handmaid to receive Him into her womb, and to give Him *natural* incarnation and birth.

Nature has never been known to be spiritual as well as mortal,—pertaining to the *soul* as well as to the body: men have not been made aware that *within* the body is a spirit body constructed from the *essences* of outer nature. Of that fact has no man any true idea. Natural impressions have been considered to pertain to the spirit, and it is supposed that at death a man puts off all connection with nature and enters upon the life of the spiritual world. The interiors of nature may be so designated; but the term cannot with truth be applied in an *absolute* sense. The Lord entered upon that plane of life we term INTERIOR nature. There, time is non-existent; state is all in all. There is no period of time more accessible to the Lord's advent than another. All time is as a minute to Him. He therefore performs His mission to humanity, at *all times* and at *all seasons*. He is no respecter of persons, all are equal in His sight, all being born with equal capabilities, and equally requiring His divine aid in the salvation of their souls. Therefore He redeems all,—He comes to all,—He makes the same manifestation of presence to all in all. But natural sense does not make equal report of His divine Presence. Some receive Him in one way, some in another; and many are not conscious of His presence at all; many have never even heard of His name, that they should believe on Him; others, having heard, deny or blaspheme Him. Is it a hard saying that Christ is as present with one as with another? Shall His presence in the soul of man be dependent upon natural knowledge, or the sense to perceive it? It is manifestly not so. Many have not the power to believe on Him that He should save them by so doing. "Who is He, Lord, that I might believe on Him?" "Thou hast both seen Him and it is He that talketh with thee." The Lord thus made knowledge of Himself to depend upon the sight being opened into nature. The Lord spake as He could be understood in some cases, but not in all. He was but rarely understood; yet He ceased not to speak in parables, "and without a parable spake He not unto them." The Lord was, however, raised from the dead; then He expounded to them the Scriptures, in such wise that their hearts burned at the hearing of His speech. The Lord is now "risen indeed, and hath appeared unto many." He hath shewed Himself unto His people that were sitting in darkness and in the shadow of death.

But we will follow our Lord after His resurrection from the sepulchre: we will speak as He spake when He expounded unto them the prophets and Scriptures concerning Himself. The Lord was made man for us that we might be men like unto Him,—that we might inherit eternal life by virtue of His manhood in us. We are then born after His image in the interiors of our life: we are so born in the interiors of our *natural* life; our bodies must, if they are to inherit eternal life, be born after His image and likeness, and under no other condition can they continue in life; we find that our earthly bodies perish, decay and pulverize; not so the body of the Lord Jesus; it saw no corruption. Yet I have shewn that no human flesh *can* be exempt from decomposition, it is the inheritance of nature. Had the Lord Jesus assumed *corporeal* flesh, as well as our sins and our infirmities, no fiat of Omnipotence could have exempted His body from the grasp of the worm that feedeth on the grain of the tomb. Had it been so, no grub could henceforth be fed by human flesh. That law would have been abrogated, as well as that which released mankind from the bonds of spiritual death—death of the germ-soul, which was the work Christ came to accomplish. In His own person, by His own arm, was that purpose effected. Germs are set at liberty,—unbound,—let go free; but, if Jesus come not to them in person, they must remain stinking in the caves of rocks: these, at His death, are rent and opened, and their tenants go up to the holy city. Jesus was in nature when He talked with Adam and with Eve; when He was called Jehovah on Mount Sinai: Jesus was His name *then* as well as Jehovah. But the Jews knew Him not under the name of Jesus. He was so called, for "He shall save His people from their sins." The Lord Jesus is then a present Saviour; He saved Israel long before the Gospel age. He saved Adam and Eve. He saves the first as well as the last. He is abiding in us, and we are abiding in Him; not by virtue of any periodical exhortation that we should so do, but by virtue of His advent into nature, which is coeval with the creation of time and of men, and of women, who are subservient unto time.

Jesus is born into the world, because it is in the world that woman can alone give birth to natural souls, and He desired to become an inmate of nature; but He did not subject Himself unto time, nor to mortal conditions. He came of a kingly ancestry,—such as Adam ere he fell from his primeval glory; and He also came of a peasant stock pertaining to Mary and her house. He came of sin, and He came of Deity. He is God and He is man. As the infinite attributes of God are finitely exhibited in man, so are the finite attributes of infinity manifest in Christ. So He unites Humanity with Divinity—Godhood with Manhood. We receive His image into our minds; we are unable to think of a multiplicity of Christs; such an idea cannot gain admittance: but, we know that Jesus is not received by one as He is by another. We are ignorant of His laws and by what means He visualizes Himself to our mental view. We know that a person named, but not seen by any number of persons, will assume a different aspect in the imagination of each; and that all their various conceptions will probably be equally untrue as a portraiture of the person to whom their thoughts have severally been directed. This is the case with the mortal conception of the Lord Christ. He is not truly represented in any of the human portraitures arising in the minds of His disciples: they each behold Him under a different aspect. Nevertheless, He is one and the same to all and each of them. He is efficient unto the salvation of each; and if it were possible for any interchange to take place, neither would possess an efficient Saviour for his peculiar individual requirements.

Thus we desire to make it appear that the epochal advent of the Lord Christ would not be efficient to redeem the sins of the whole world; but the *perpetual* advent is so. God in the flesh is ever present; He is in the flesh *now*; He is so revealed by prophet and evangelist; He is so written of by psalmist and historian. Christ is the PRESENT GOD; we are children of nature; so is He a babe of nature,—growing with our growth, increasing with our stature, imbuing us with supernatural wisdom, whereby we attain unto favor with God and man; and, in His light we see light. He is the "light of the world," and it shineth upon *every* man in the world.

Men have not thought of how these things could be; neither have they thought how anything could be that did not come before their eyes. The disciple Thomas has been believed to be a man like unto one of us; but there are sceptics without number; all are Thomas: he is manifest in nature, and we need not go far to find him. The Lord Christ is in nature, and if we seek we shall find Him also, He tells us, ever knocking at the door; if we will open that door He will come in and will sup with us, and we with Him. How should that be, if He *once* did so with His disciples in a way that cannot *now* be? Would that we had lived in that age, when we might have received the Lord into our homes, and given Him meat from our boards! Say not so, blind natural sense! The Lord Jesus was never more *naturally* present in a past age, than He is *at this day*. He is in the interior of thy being,—thou art living and moving in Him,—thou art drawing spiritual breath with the breath of nature, even because the Lord Christ is in nature,—has allowed Himself to be born of its substance,—carried in its womb, conceived in its iniquity; taken upon Himself our "coat of skin," that it might be no hindrance to our attainment of eternal life. In His flesh-advent we live, move, and have our being; we are temples for the Holy Spirit to dwell in,—we are Christ-temples,—Christians, not all nominally so, but one and all *vitally* so. There is but one God; Christ is His natural impersonation: there is but one Christ, one Almighty Saviour. The fact of His being born of every human being in the world, does not part Him into separate identities; that conception may be unavoidable to the natural mind, contemplating Deity in the flesh from its own standpoint. Man is Adam, woman is Eve; man is Joseph in his *inner* being,—in that life which takes *no part* in nature; woman is Mary, in that part of *interior life* which can contribute to the birth of Christ into nature. Feminine humanity is the natural parent of the Lord Jesus; she produces a babe, having been herself born into that estate; she gives birth to the Lord. Generations yet unborn will do so. He is in the *past, present,* and *future*; He is the first and also the last: "who *is* and who was to come," the ever-present God and Lord.

But finite sense comprehendeth Him not; it cannot see in the light of interior nature, it is dazzled, blinded, confused. It saith, "How can such things be?" That they can be is not yet able to be clearly demonstrated: all that can be given is now written, and it sufficeth unto the day; more, much more, may come, but it is not good to anticipate. Let us live in the present, being sure that the future will be equally well provided for.

Woman has taught man wisdom, and has opened

blind eyes; not by means of individual womanhood has it been effected: woman, in the collective sense of the term, has been efficient unto this end,—chosen for this almighty purpose; and, if we regard the mission allotted to woman throughout the holy records, we shall not be slow to hear this word. She came into life for man; she continues to live for him; she ministers to his every necessity, be it natural or spiritual: she is hence in the office of Christ; she is identified with Christ, as having contributed to His advent into nature; she bears His cross upon her breast; she lives her life in His. Not one woman only has done this; all women are doing so, not one more than another. The harlot Rahab can save the city as well as the chaste wife, but not perceptibly. She who writes does so under a veil that is not penetrable even to herself; be it far from her to desire to raise it! rather let its folds be thickened around her earthly form: and let no man gaze on her as she is seen of God. Let not her sisters call her "highly favored," for they are in the like case; they are one and all employed in this mission, for it had its rise in Eden. It is for woman to shew forth the Lord Christ Jesus; it is for Him to be made manifest in and by His second creation, woman. Let this observation stand in its place, and if its import be not yet apparent, it will be, as time and revelation advance. The Christian dispensation is progressive, but never reaches a climax; it may pause in its development at certain epochs, then progress with renewed vigour, but stationary it can never be.

———

Christ in heaven is not the Christ that is worshipped in the temples of misconception that men have built up for themselves to worship in; neither is God the same there that is worshipped in heaven, nor is the Holy Spirit the same divine person that men recognize in their adorations of an image which Nebuchadnezzar the king hath set up, that God's own sons should bow down to. That is not a God that can deliver you out of the fire of evil lust; but the one person seen with Shadrach, Meshach, and Abednego; He is in the likeness of the Son of Man, and He will walk at your side when you are in the furnace of affliction prepared for you by the king of the world, whose idolatry you will not heed. The Scripture text is full of hidden meaning: let it appear, and men will look into the furnace they themselves have enkindled, and will behold the likeness of the Son of Man walking therein. The shadow of Jesus is visible to my spiritual sight in every line of Holy Writ; in that temple I do not see the ministering priests: I only see the God I worship,—in likeness a man, in belongings a woman;—in the microscope an infinitesimal unit, in the telescope a Being my utmost vision cannot compass. In all these differences of outward appearing do I behold God defined in Scripture; the whole of which, from Genesis to Revelation, treats exclusively of Him, of His attributes, of His parts and passions, and of His inner and outer dealings with men.

This being the case, it is not for me to take up Scripture here and lay it down there; but it is for me to define in what manner the whole is to be made to cohere together; to seam it into one garment wherewith to cover the body of Christ: so that if it be despoiled, it must be rent asunder, but cannot be unripped.

If a man proclaim truth upon a housetop, to the wounding of some tender spirit who has not as yet the ability to receive it, he is a thief, for he has stolen that which is not his, till it is given him by God to scatter abroad and to distribute. Christ healed the afflicted, and said unto them, "See that thou tell no man." Why not?—for then others might have come unto Him. But they had better not come till He shall call them,—till He shall see that it is time to go unto Lazarus.

The Jewish people ministered unto their own necessities, they sought for outward manifestation of internal truth. They mourned over the downfall of their nation, and they sought comfort in the hope and in the prospect of a deliverance from bondage, and an exalter of themselves in the person of the promised Messiah. They were a rebellious and a stiff-necked people, but a people that would adhere strictly to the fulfilment of the Decalogue as it had been brought down to them by Moses, who was to them in the place of God,—in the place of that God who came down to them in form a Man, and in very deed, the God whom angels worship. "If ye say, We see, ye shall have the greater condemnation," said Christ. The Divine Being does not consider any step a false one, if it will lead a soul nearer to Himself. Obedience may be required in trivialities as well as in weighty matters, and the principle will be alike operative, perhaps, more so in one case than in the other; but it will be accordingly, a blind or an enlightened obedience.

The Jewish ritual was one of types and shadows, yet one of deep internal import. It was of the same internal significance to the Jew that the sacramental rites of baptism and the Holy Supper are to the Christian now,—mystic ceremonies that have no intrinsic meaning, but which are yet the emblems of regeneration and sanctification through and by the birth and death of Christ.

The upright Jew had no regenerator and no sanctifier but Jesus, whom he called Messiah when he thought of God by anticipation, and Jehovah when present to His mind. He had no scribe to read to him the law of God as it is engraved upon the heart, but only as it was written by the finger of Moses, *after the first tables were broken.* He required a God to worship, or else how was he to attain salvation? He required to obey, but had no master to serve; He would bow down to idols rather than have no God to worship, and to bring sacrifice unto. God loved the righteous Jew, and He loves Him still. God does not consider the Jew an outcast; but He desires to bring him into the holy city, with the Jew of the New Jerusalem. Jesus provided for the Israelite of old, as He provides for the children He is leading into Canaan now. The Canaan that is seen of men, and the Canaan that is inhabited by the spirits of just men made perfect, is one and the same land; one is the body, the other the spirit. The land of Canaan is ever flowing with milk and with honey. To this land will Jew and Gentile come, when the Jew sees his Messiah in Christ Jesus; the Gentile his idol; and the Christian his one God.

Simeon is saying that Christ shall be for the fall and for the rising again of many in Israel,—that a sword shall pass through Mary also, that the thoughts of many hearts may be revealed. Oh! how piercing is the shriek that resounds through nature's chambers when the truth comes forth to view! How many knew not to what it was leading them! that they must see *their* Son—*their* God crucified—in order to see Him rise! How mystical the words of Simeon, yet how true!

That the Scripture cannot be broken is a rule we must never lose sight of; but that it must be fulfilled within our souls, is a truth that must be responded to by every male that openeth the womb, for the child Jesus to issue forth that He may be seen of men.

The God Christ Jesus is not here and not there.

He is not in the heaven of the old dispensation and in the world of the new; but He is in heaven, in the earth, in the hells, and in the spirit of princes; in the babe and in the womb of woman about to bring forth in His image and likeness.

When the understanding speaks, the affections listen. The affections are divided into many and various degrees of relationship to the understanding. They are, if all is well, controlled by the understanding; and they render it a willing and a delighted obedience. They do not desire to minister to themselves, but to be always directed in offices by the controlling power of the understanding that dwells in the same house with them. If the understanding be deficient in directing ability, the affections are dismayed and retire to the chamber of the will, which not being the guardian appointed them by God, they are led astray, and perversion and all disorder of the mental functions ensues. But, when the understanding is in a healthy state,—inspiring and respiring according to the law of life God has enacted for it, then is peace and plenty within the house, and the soul's cornucopia is filled with fruit and flowers.

The prophetess Anna must serve the Lord without ceasing. She was of a great age and was a widow, having no husband to direct her course. She had, however, lived with one for seven years from her virginity. But why are we informed of these particulars; for what does it concern us to know them? Yet there is no jot or tittle of the law that shall be lightly esteemed by us;—no link of this chain can be broken without the falling of the vessel by which I am drawing up the water of truth out of this unfathomable well.

The woman who had lived but seven years with an husband from her virginity, is like unto the woman who had seven husbands from her virginity, yet, the last clause of the sentence is not used in the one case as in the other. It would be just as true to apply it to one case as to the other; yet it must not be said of the woman who had seven husbands, but it must be said of the woman who ministered night and day in the temple, and departed not thence. When the affection for the Lord leads the soul to be devoted to *His* service only, then it is a virgin affection, for it knoweth none other; but it was not so from the beginning, for it had an husband seven years,—passing through that week which Rachel had to fulfil before she could be given to Jacob who loved her so much. The affections will serve the world, if the world claim them; but when that is withdrawn they will serve the Lord night and day, who is then become an husband unto them.

John the Baptist was in the wilderness until the day of his shewing unto Israel: his meat was locusts and wild honey; his clothing, camel's hair with a girdle of skin. In this respect, John was different to his brethren of the flesh; he did not eat as they did, he did not dwell in a house as they did; neither are we told that he pitched a tent in the wilderness in which he sojourned: but "he was in the wilderness till the day of his shewing unto Israel." Was he not also in the wilderness when he shewed himself unto Israel, and when they came out of the towns and the villages to be baptized of him? Where was John then, if not on Jordan's bank in the wilderness? Yes, —he—John, was in the *wilderness of spirit* when he baptized on the banks of Jordan, for Jordan is now overflowing his banks in our midst. Jordan is typical of natural regeneration, when the Lord appears as a man coming to be baptized of John in the waters of a natural river, not partaking of the baptism of fire which He was afterwards baptized with. John is *now* baptizing at Jordan's bank, because there is much water there, and Jesus is *now* and *ever* coming to be baptized there; because He will fulfil every tittle of the law in order that the children of the wilderness may see God, and that He may be a light to lighten the Gentiles, and be the glory of His people Israel. He is so doing when a babe is brought unto Him in the way of presentation that is now extant in the world. When it wails, Jesus is soothing it by the descent of the dove of His Divine power; —when it is an unconscious recipient of divine gifts; —when it feels the baptismal water on its brow, Jesus is making the cross upon its soul.

This is the baptism of John, that ye bring forth much fruit; but by what means is not known. It seems as though it came unsought and unasked for, even as the babe asks not to be baptized; so neither does the Gentile spirit; but repentance comes even as a dove that was not expected to descend upon the Son of Man when He riseth out of the waters of Jordan. He—the Son of Man—will be as other men to the simple in heart; for He will pray, and be unto them as a brother; but to the strong in strife, He will be the Son of the living God,—the Christ who was to come forth of the family of David,—of the house and lineage of Jesse.

The family of Jesse was descended from the posterity of Adam by a long line of ancestors; they are recorded in the order of genealogy from the reputed father of Christ, and not from His true parent, Mary. What then has Christ to do with this long line of progenitors which we find enumerated in the Scripture account of the birth of Jesus into nature? The birth of Christ was on this wise, and the birth of John was on this wise, because the two are united in their respective callings. John is the Christ who came to the Jews in the first place, for he preached repentance and the remission of sins; he also baptized with water, which is a natural element. Fire is a spiritual one. There are in the world elements of nature and elements of spirit. Fire is a spiritual substance sufficiently gross to become assimilated with natural light, that it can be perceptible to the natural senses.

It is a certain law existing in nature, that natural appearances shall be produced by natural means; but it does not therefore follow that the appearance produced is natural. The nature of water is quite opposite to that of fire; it will in no case assimilate with it. Hence we may now perceive why we are first to be baptized with water, and afterwards with fire. We must first receive natural truth, and afterwards spiritual;—we must first be instructed as a child, and then, when we can put away childish things, we shall be enabled to receive that which pertaineth unto manhood. When we are baptized with water, we are in the wilderness, and Jordan will afford us the baptismal fluid; for Jordan is overflowing all his banks when the ark is passing over, and when the feet of the Levites touch his waters, he will stand up as an heap on either side of that holy sanctuary which the hand of man must not be careless to handle; for the Lord's is the arm that can alone support it.

Jordan's waters are the pure yet simple loves of childhood and of early youth; and, it may be, that many an aged Christian still loves the waters of innocence that take not the ark of God on their surface, but let it pass through their minds; being content to know that there is such a holy thing, and not desiring to touch it.

This is the state of her who is now writing for me. I am bringing down into her mind an angelic presence, and she only desires that her natural fallacies of perception may retire, in order to make way for the truths she perceives I have the ability to bear unto the other side of her Jordan. She is not aware of any effort in thus removing her natural mind from contact with that which is spiritual,—too much so for it to comprehend,—because she has previously placed her soul in the hand of Him who can bid the intellectual faculty proper to her sphere to stand up as an heap on either side, while I, the priest of God, bring His ark through those now silent waters.

But this is a condition of the will which must be experienced by every mind desiring to understand the truth contained in these revealments; for they are not written for the natural, but for the spiritual mind. The natural mind has been cared for in previous communications.* The Man of sorrows has cared for it, and He so typified His care for the child of nature when He was baptized of John in the waters of Jordan; for John said, "I have need to be baptized of thee, and comest thou to me?" Jesus said, "Suffer it to be so now, for thus it becometh us to fulfil all righteousness." It also becometh us to fulfil all the righteousness of nature ere we go into the depths of spirit-perception which we shall find dawning upon us, when we have been baptized with the Holy Spirit of fire.

Jesus must increase, John must decrease: natural religion must be superseded by spiritual religion; appearances of truth must give place to realities of truth. John must be in the wilderness until the

* *An Angel's Message.*

day of his shewing unto Israel, which is a day that is *now* dawning. John eats locusts and wild honey; Christ turns water into wine, when there is a marriage in Cana of Galilee. There is a marriage *now;* and *now* is the water of Jordan standing up as an heap, while the ark of the covenant of spiritual truth is passing through on the dry land.

There is joy in heaven over one sinner that repenteth, more than over the ninety and nine just persons who need no repentance; wherefore, bring forth fruit meet for repentance, and say not "we have Abraham to our father, for I say unto you, God is able of these stones to raise up children unto Abraham." In the case of the wilful sinner, fruit must be brought, fit for repentance; that is, good works must be done, and offerings of the affections made on the altar of self-sacrifice: but, in the case of hereditary sin, an offering by fire must be made, that it may be meet for the required repentance; like unto Abraham when he was told to offer up his miraculously-born son, Isaac. God had raised up Isaac unto Abraham by the power of the cornerstone of the temple of truth, that stone being Jesus who was about to baptize with fire. Out of these stones,—those of the new dispensation, can God in Christ raise up children, or principles of righteousness that shall minister to the requirements of His people, at which Jacob shall rejoice and Israel shall be glad.

The children which God could raise up out of

these stones unto Abraham, are the works of God not made with human hands, any more than was Isaac's body made of Sarah's substance, for she had none wherewith to make it. It was a work of God performed by Himself alone, without the co-operation of natural law. The works which God will plant in the heart, are those which will spring forth into activity by the clear shining of the stones of holy truth. These are the spiritual children who will save you, for they have the mystery of the old dispensation of Abraham for their father, or for their stone of truth; yet these will not serve you, if you bring not likewise forth the works meet for repentance which the John,—the forerunner of the new dispensation of righteousness requires; for, he also was of miraculous conception,—a type of that holy spiritual principle which must be implanted in the natural mind by the power of God, ere the spiritual principle can be raised up.

"The Holy Ghost was not yet given, because that Jesus was not yet glorified;" the Holy Spirit can never be given till Jesus is glorified.

This is the God to whom nothing is impossible, to whom nature is but a tool wherewith to mould and fashion the souls and bodies of men; this is the Holy Spirit who can now overshadow whom He pleaseth, for " His people shall be willing in the day of His power." But He tempereth His east wind to the shorn lamb of His flock: so He now removeth the veil that conceals the glory and the power of His aspect, by the gradual and careful tending of one and many of His ministers above. He knoweth that the natural frame is weak,—He knoweth that it hath need of rest, and He saith, "Sleep on now and take your natural repose, for the time of strife draweth nigh."

One dispensation is not at variance with another dispensation, but all are bound together into one indissoluble bond of union. There are many representations of God, but one and the same God. There are many forms of revealed religion, but one and the same faith. There are many mansions, but one and the same heaven, or house of God. The Holy Spirit is the proceeding power of God. It cannot cease to proceed from Him: if it did, there could be no universe, no creation, no dispensation of light to Jew or Gentile, no manifestation of the power of God in nature or in spirit-life.

The gift of the Holy Spirit is identical with the power of God to procreate human beings to receive it. It is not given to one and withheld from another; but it descends upon the devil as well as upon the angel, and upon every intermediate condition of life. It moveth upon dark waters, and upon bright and shining ones. It rideth upon the storm and flieth upon the whirlwind, and it broodeth over the placid lake of the soul. It is not here nor there, but everywhere. It melteth the stony heart that it may become a heart of flesh; and it poureth oil and wine into the wound of the earthly traveller. It is the good Samaritan who will pay two pence for the healing of his brother's sores; and it will come again to see if more can be done for the sufferers of earth. It is the star of the east guiding wise men to the lap of truth, where they will find the young child, who will hold out His hands, to them even as He will when they are laden with the spiritual blessings He alone can bestow. This is the Holy Spirit of truth that shall guide you into all truth. This is the Comforter; this is the baptism of fire with which every Christian shall be baptized.

APPENDIX.

SELECTIONS

FROM

SPIRITUAL WRITINGS.

REPRINTED FROM "THE DAWN."

DIVINE MINISTRATIONS IN NATURE.

The Lord is good to all. All are provided for in His unerring counsels. The man of low stature must have a tree to climb up into ere he can behold the Lord even in His natural humanity. A flower may grow and flourish in nature, though a gardener does not tend it, and it is not cared for by the hand that will gather it, and then cast it to the winds, which will in their turn waft it into the path of some little one, who will say, "Oh! what a sweet flower is this!" So it is with the blossoms of truth that are cast on the world, with this exception, that the natural flower will fade while the flowers of the Spirit will survive over the night, and be fresher in the morning than when first gathered from their bed of development. The Lord is a refiner of silver; He will watch over the process of refinement, and will then mould it for His own purposes. He will make of it instruments of use and of beauty also. Molten silver is not more easily formed into the shape of beauty designed for it by the natural artificer, than is the spirit of man prepared for heaven, when all the desires of the soul are relinquished into the hand of God, who can then conform them into perfect accordance with His own divine desires. And it is by this conformity of natural with holy and spiritual desires, that a state of celestial harmony is produced, and peace is made to reign within the mind. We may experience a desire to attain unto a more refined and higher degree of spirituality, but it will not arise from any anxiety on the subject; it will simply be the outpouring of the Divine love which will reach the outer consciousness as a desire to be still more fully centred in the midst of that ever-flowing stream of living water which springs forth from Himself alone, and it will also manifest itself in an ever-increasing desire to be made the means of use, comfort, and enlightenment to others,—to all who come within our immediate presence, and also, if possible, to diffuse abroad the good things that have so bountifully been bestowed upon ourselves. Then will come the petition, "Lord, give unto me that I may give again to him that hath the need of that which thou hast to give in great abundance." And who ever asked of God in vain when the desire to ask was prompted by Himself? Do we need to know how it is that we are led by slow degrees nearer and nearer unto Himself? Let us see into what chamber He will lead us, in order to shew us the beauty and harmony of the whole natural structure which He has caused to be reared up even unto the clouds, and to rise into the unseen regions of spirit that are by them concealed from our view.

Our Lord places a babe upon the earth; He gives it a

parent that cares not for it; it was born in sin and conceived in iniquity,—externally as well as internally defiled by the tendency to sin which every child of Adam inherits from the fact of evil having entered into nature by and through his fall. Yet God is gracious—is love itself to all, to the world's outcast and to its son of admiration also. His eye detects the sentiment—the thought that dare not—cannot be as yet elevated to Himself. The garment of preservation from the rough winds of earth is cast by the hand of Omnipotence over the weak and shivering soul. Mortal eye sees it not, the mortal on whose soul it falls feels it not. The babe was nurtured in vice, was never told of any world beyond the one it looks out on with the eye of flesh. But it hears the church bell,—it sees other little ones going and their parents leading them, and it sees that they are cared for, and that Sunday is a day of rest, that morning and evening prayers are said, that there is a something going on within the building that rises up so high above the courts of dull and gloomy aspect, wherein his little head is pillowed when the day of rest is past,—something that now and then bursts forth in a pleasant sound to which he loves to listen, for the love of sweet sound is implanted deep in every human breast. And why? Because it is a powerful means wherewith to work out man's salvation. Gentle is the hand that guides where gentleness is needed, and strong is the blast that will blow down the pinnacle of self-exaltation when it rises on the pedestal of self-imaginings. When the child thinks how sweet is the sound of the organ, that comes forth from a sanctuary his little feet have never trod, who shall say what sanctuary has been opened within his own soul? What passion staid in its course,—what headlong torrent intercepted? What cham-

her window opened for the light and warmth of heaven to enter in at? God would not have made the heart of man to rejoice in the bright sunshine, to sport in the green field, to be thoughtful in the deep forest, and to be influenced on all occasions as the outward aspect of nature seems to impel him, but for a great purpose of his own. The mind of man, —of the peasant and of the prince alike,—is very open to the influence of nature. Nature is a very comprehensive term, and is not confined to the exhibition of trees and flowers, rock and stream; nature is visible in the church porch, in the stately mansion, in the gay colour. Nature, and her accompanying influences, will affect the human soul whether we live in her courts that are made with hands, or in those that are fashioned fresh from the hand of nature's God. The sight, the hearing, every natural sense, is a door through which the angels of heaven can pass and re-pass on their missions of love and guardianship to the soul that is committed to their charge. The angels watch over a little child. The earthly mother tends his body, and the ministering spirit tends his soul. The one puts on his little garments at the same time that the other places a guard before the tempter of the spirit. The mother who would draw her son from the path that is crossed by a serpent, is not more watchful than is the angelic guardian who is quick to perceive the wile of an evil being desirous to draw his soul into sin by the power of some unknown fascination. The great and conspicuous events of life,—the lingering wear of time on the mortal combat,—the protracted strife of tongues,—the rise and fall of dynasties and empires,—the vain caprice of custom, and the wild vagaries of fashion, are all bounded and circumscribed by a law that is far beyond the control or even of the ken of man.

Thy heart may indite a good matter, and an evil wile may overthrow it; yet thou shalt in nowise lose thy reward, for purity is purity still, though impurity may succeed in washing it away from the sight of men. Nation sins against nation, and national rights become invaded; horror, dismay, widowhood and orphanhood, follow in the train of a just intervention of power,—of power delegated from God to man. Oppression has dared to raise up its swollen head, and magnanimity has taken up the sword of right to demonstrate that religion and piety reign in the land. But whence the cry of anguish from a broken heart? Why do we see the virtuous wife torn from her husband's arms, and the little one from its mother's breast? Because there *is* a God that rules over the right and over the wrong; for the timid one is made strong, and the stony heart may be melted when the stroke has fallen, and the revengeful blow has laid both suppliant and supplicated low in the dust of earth. When both arise from nature's clay, who shall say what vile passion may lie buried there? Who shall say what distortion of the natural brain may have obscured the light of spirit-essence that would otherwise have shone forth on the hideous deed, and staid the murderer's hand? Be that as it may, is there no hope for the man we gaze on in the dress of humanity that is exposed to the rough winds of the world? And may not the rents and seams we behold so plainly, be caused by the world's rough usage? "Many are called but few are chosen." May not this passage breathe divine favour upon *all?* The *few* are not those that alone go in to the marriage supper of the Lamb; they are those who have always sat at His feet; but the *called* are those to whom He has to raise His voice, so that it may be heard in the dark places of the earth, that the graves may yield up their dead, and that the dead in nature may live and have their bones shaken, and be vivified by the breath of heaven.

Many are called, and many hear and will hear that divine call. But woe unto him that stayeth his coming until he shall hear it. The Lord does not break; but with a strong hand and with an ever out-stretched arm, He bends. Soft and tender is the bending to some, and very hard and terribly painful to others,—to the "called out of Edom," —to the deaf ears, stern will be the voice, but they could not hear if it were soft. The "chosen" are sitting at His feet; to them His *whisper* is audible. They have chosen that good part which nothing can take from them. But they love not more than those to whom much has been forgiven. Those who, when safe within their Father's house, will look back upon the stony path they trod, and see how they have been led, in what dark nights the pillar of fire went before them, and the cloud guided them in the day of nature, and their murmurings were pardoned, and how they were sustained in the wilderness they passed with so much doubt and fear. Bread came, and water came at the decree of God, and so also came the quail and the locust.

So comes now the wind and the calm,—the cloud and the rain,—the flower and the fruit,—the bird and the insect. Not of themselves they come,—appear and disappear,— exist and non-exist,—not by any once decreed law of creation, irrespective of the everchanging states of human beings, but by an immutable law and ordinance of God, fixed indeed by His decree, but wholly dependent upon His first and grandest creation—man. Man derives his breath —natural as well as spiritual—by virtue of his constant relation to his Maker. He is not made and then thrown off, as it were, from his Creator, but he is ever attached to Him by a ligature that is never—can never—be dissevered. The stream of life is ever flowing forth fresh and renewed from the Divine Fount. Nature is dependent upon men; that is, did not man exist, nature could not exist either: the one is dependent upon the other. It follows from these premises, that man and nature are alike a spontaneous outpouring of the Divine power to create living as well as inanimate forms, portraitures of His own Divine idea. It also follows that the *motion* of all the animal and vegetable kingdoms must be adapted to the particular requirements of man, since he is the superior creation, and it is a law that is universally recognized, even by the natural intellect alone, that the greater shall be ministered unto by the lesser. Consequently plants grow, animals move, birds fly, the air transmits sound and odours in its impalpable texture, just in that one order of proceeding that is required for the transmission of some message of interior import, to call forth some buried remembrance, or to produce some particular state of feeling that is to subserve a Divine end. And the Divine Being has, and can have no other end in view, in all that He does, but to promote the ultimate salvation and blessing of the human race.

The human spirit is the continent whereon subsist all that can be called spiritual. The stone cannot contain a spiritual principle within it in the degree that man can. But it can portray the existence of that principle to the human mind; it is an out-birth and natural consequence of the existence of that which is intangible within the breast of man; and it can minister to his spiritual and natural requirements at one and the same time. Thus a stone that has lain for centuries in the bosom of the earth, was made and prepared for the building of a temple in which man is to worship and adore his Maker and the Maker of the stone as well. Did man not require the use of temples made with stone, would it be so prepared for him? Is not the requirement identical with the production? And is not the spiritual principle in man, which leads him to worship God, a primary principle founded upon his immortal nature? Thus it is that the external nature is all dependent upon the requirements of the internal nature; and, did man not need to repose his faith upon a pillar of stone, no stone would exist.

The mind of man is complex in construction, and in its continuous action. It may be of a spiritual, or it may be of a merely rational development. In either case it awakens spiritual affinity with spiritual beings. The rational man who is not spiritually minded, is as near to the spiritual world as he who is of a true spiritual genius. But the natural rational man is of a very different degree of affinity to God from that of the spiritual man. The one is His elder, the other His younger son; one is nigh unto Him, the other is further off, and will have to be drawn into His sphere by cords of love which He will provide for that purpose.

The man of a purely rationalistic mind is wholly engrossed by the things of sense that belong to the body, the world, its government, and laws. He thinks himself wise in his generation; and so he is, in that respect he is wiser than the children of light. But the poor peasant, or the skilful artizan—how is it with them? They toil not neither do they know of the garments of heaven, yet are they weaving them each one for himself, spinning them on the spindle of time, and weaving them in the woof of nature. But the rational and the learned in their day, who heed not the learning of the skies, but walk the earth with the head cast down as the beast of burden that bears them on their earthly path,—they may not have the sin that destroyeth, but neither have they the garment that will admit to the sanctuary of God. They have not spun it, so it cannot be produced. Yet they shall in no case lose their reward; provision is made for them in the courts of heaven. But unless the King of heaven be acknowledged, no entrance into His kingdom can be obtained. How then can this acknowledgment be drawn from them? for they have not cultivated the spiritual faculties. Were they to be told,—" You must be found perfect in all worldly science," they would be joyful; for then all their earthly riches would be available for their own exaltation. But when they are told,—" Such things are of no use here; you must part with these and follow the cross of Christ, which can alone lead you to the heaven you desire to enter,"—they are very sad and go away sorrowful.

Thus it is that the rich in worldly knowledge, though poor in spiritual wisdom, prepare for themselves much trouble and vexation of spirit; for if the spirit of a man be not adapted to the life it must enter upon when the gate of nature is closed, how can he be happy? It is not for the lack of information or means to acquire the knowledge of spiritual laws, because they are placed before every human being according to his capacity to receive; but it is that the inclination to study them has been wanting,—husks have been chosen instead of bread. Had the husk been put aside when the bread was offered, celestial knowledges would have risen on the foundation of nature.

But, as it is, the rich young man goes sorrowfully away, for he has great possessions that are not now of any value, being only a clog upon the wheels of the chariot that is to bear him into the presence of God and His angels. This feeling of heaviness will, however, cause those chariot wheels to move. They are now anointed with the oil of heaven, for the man has been withdrawn a step from his former vain imaginings,—and so much hindrance and dismay will his useless worldly acquisitions cause him to experience in the life he has now entered, that he will himself remove them out of the way to his eternal home, and he will again seek knowledge in a new school, for he has now learnt that the former things pass away, and he will desire to acquire that which will not pass away, but endure unto everlasting life. Hence it is that there are heavenly instructors and wise teachers, and professors of angelic sciences in the world that is within, yet above, the world of nature.

And where will all this instruction and spiritual preparation for the heavens take place? In a plane of the creation that does not come within the range of natural vision, a land that is neither heaven nor hell, in a court or antechamber, with doors leading in opposite directions,—leading into opposite kingdoms,—the one leading to the kingdom of light,—the other to that of darkness. Consequently, the inhabitants of both kingdoms can there find access; malevolence and hate invite to one route,—and love, devotion, and pity to the other. The mass of mankind will turn to the guardian angel at their side, and will say, " I will go with you;" but if the spirit so turning is untrue to his inward inclination,—if he love evil, and delight in the exercise of impure propensities, he will find that no step can be taken in the right direction; so that no progress can possibly be made towards heaven till the unclean thing has been removed from the chariot wheel that is within the breast. There is wheel within wheel, and the living creature is within the wheels.

Many think they can strike out a much better path for themselves than the one into which they are directed by God, and then both the way and the goal are alike productive of pain and unrest. The self-directed spirit is dismayed by false alarms, and the soul trusting in God is continually calm. The trusting spirit has no fears for the future, and no anxious hope; for it lives in the present, and knows not what a day may be bring forth.

It lives *spiritually*, not *carnally*; it mourns over no imimpediment to its peace, for it suffers none to exist. It puts not up the barrier that exists only in its own imagining; for it knows that God arranges for to-day and for to-morrow also. This is the secret of heavenly felicity. The angels do not dwell on the future; they do not reflect how much happier they shall be as their states progress; nor do they mourn over the trials of their friends on earth, because they know that God is just, and that none suffer without a cause, and without a purpose. A purpose God hath in all that He doeth and causeth to come to pass in the world. That purpose cannot be interfered with; if it could be changed by our chafing, eternal misery must be the result. Therefore let us consider our words and our actions, for God acts not without a purpose,—that of promoting our eternal blessedness. Let us not chafe at the apparent roughness of our path, for if we will walk steadily in it, we shall find it is the only one we *can* walk in that will lead us to heaven.

We ought not to pray for our *own will* to be accomplished, for it is a vain thing, and is altogether lighter than vanity. Rather should we pray for sorrow, if sorrow will purify us from earthly taint; or for the grief of heart that will remove its cause. We should earnestly desire that the holy will of God be done, and ask not what that will is, in order that we may be happy in the present life, or even in that which is to come. We should long that our will may be transformed into the will of God,—that we may be the images of Him who has made us all to be as "children of light," taking the reflection of His pristine ray, some receiving it in one way, and some in another; some being as the green herb, some as the blue heaven, some as the red flame, some as the yellow gold, and some as the pure crystal. The humble seeker after the will of God is often tossed to and fro on the troubled sea of life ere he is taken from the shell which has served to form him into the semblance of a precious pearl,—into a receptacle of light divine. Let the sea roar and the fulness thereof, but let our soul be as the pearl that is sheltered and secure, till it is taken out of the troubled waters.

Providence does not work any work by chance, or for an indifferent or unimportant object, but every event of time and circumstance is under particular as well as general direction, and continual supervision. If we are to be employed in the fulfilment of a particular use on a certain day, no natural event can possibly occur to prevent us in the accomplishment of that duty. Even if it be a seeming trifle or pleasure that we propose to take part in, nothing can hinder its accomplishment, if eternal ends are dependent thereon. So all the comings in and goings out of our lives are regulated by an unerring hand, and although we are in all cases to act as if we could control the wind and the waves of time, yet must we stop at the decree, "so far shalt thou go and no further." Let us not, therefore, seek to penetrate into the events, nor enquire on what thread the scales of our life are suspended. They are in the Hand that can alone balance them aright, and if it were possible for them to be swayed by the human will, destruction and spiritual death must be the inevitable consequence.

In the great and more striking outlines of life, this rule of Divine Providence is the most apparent, and is not so discernible in the faint shadows that fill up the interstices. Yet those who recognize the divine Artist in the one, will not fail to do so in the other. They will reflect that it is all the work of one hand,—that the design and the execution have alike sprung from the same source. Beautiful things are said to come from God, and pleasant times and seasons are acknowledged to be regulated by Him. Summer is thought to be the perfection of beauty, and so it is, for then in their brightness and power are all the sweet and holy emblems of purity and love, and the flying fowl of the air are in the fulness of joy, and all creation is redolent with life. Desolation and gloom wait till the morrow, yet the same Almighty hand regulates the summer, and the winter also. The same eye beholds the smile and also the tear. God is in the storm and in the calm alike,—in the sunshine and in the shade. Nay, do you not sometimes feel His presence more palpably in the darkness than in the light? He is covering us from the heat that might burn up the green herb of the soul, and when we see others sport in the sunshine, let us say within ourselves, "The Lord waiteth to be gracious unto me also, but I know not the season thereof." How might the torn breast become healed if this balm of Gilead were thus applied! But it is not for us to heal the suffering heart, nor to stay its palpitations in natural life; we can only endeavor to smooth the rough places of ascent towards the one universal home of mortality. Let us not behold our Lord under one aspect alone. Let us not follow Him into the synagogue and not through the cornfield as well. Let us sit with Him on the mount, and in the ship also. Let us be with Him in the breaking of bread, and at His side in the wilderness. Let us be at the cross, and at the sepulchre early in the morning. Let our affections rise with Him to the realms that are above our natural sight, and let us in spirit behold Him come again near unto us, though it be in the clouds of a dim natural vision that has not yet cast off the scales of mortality.

Nature is but the prelude to spirit, and spiritual perception will ascend on the wing of eternity. Time is passing, and eternity is passing too. Yes,—now, in the day of the world, eternity is progressing, and states have commenced within the breast of every human being from which the future conditions of the spirit are to be developed. Heaven is opening or heaven is closing upon every mortal being that walks the earth, where the mortal combat is waged,—death or life. Put up the sacred banner and cry,—"I will have peace on earth only when it is a holy peace. I will not have the peace of indifference to the interests of the country I would call my own, to the destruction of that which can alone sanction my claim to possess the land of my birth-promise, a land flowing with milk and honey, of which I can never taste if I fight not the battle of life in the armor which God has Himself prepared for me." Beloved, say this in the recesses of your souls; whisper it in the secret chamber and be not afraid to proclaim it upon the house-top. Proclaim aloud that your strength is in the living God, in whose name you sustain continual combat with degenerate foes who love not the land whose every stone is so dear to you. Far and near let this note of the clarion be heard, by the strong man and by the weaker organ of the babe in spirit. Modulate its tone to the tender one. Put it up in its case when the time to sound is not, and quickly draw it forth when the occasion and the hour require. Let those who know the melody of the spheres never be slow to point out where it may be heard, and let those who would desire to hear listen to the entreaties of others who love them sincerely. Do not say, "I cannot see as he sees, I cannot hear as he hears." Who first told him that the skies sent forth a sound that he had never heard before? Who but God told him that? And who but God can tell you? His voice may reach your spirit also. You may not hear as others hear; you can only hear as you have been formed to hear. All have the power to hear the Word of the Lord, and all that hear may live.

Let us be calm in our prayers, in our aspirations, in our contemplations of eternal realities. Let not hope or fear turn the scales in which we weigh immortal gifts. Put in the treasure and ask God to weigh it for us, and mark well the turning. We will not roughly handle the heavenly down that descends to earth, sent forth by the breath of spirit to float upon a natural atmosphere; it is very soft and yielding in the winds of earth, but is able to form a firm pillow of repose for the spiritual head to rest on when the storm of life is raging.

The worm feeds on the mulberry leaf, and spins its web for itself alone; it heeds not the care with which human beings are watching it. May we not be as that loathsome thing, yet watched over by celestial beings of whose existence we are ignorant? May not the web we spin be as important to them as that of the grub to us? And are not both watched over by an Almighty eye? The grub, and the animal that works for the service of man; the man, and the spirit, the angel and archangel, are all working-tools in the hand that has no maker. They are guided by the arm that upholds the planets in their course, and sustains the babe at its mother's breast, and works out the plan of an immortal life in that tiny workshop. The same Divine Being casts a straw in our path, that it may direct our attention from the pursuit of that which He sees will harden our heart. A bird flits across our view, and we pause to reflect thereon. A serpent falls upon our bed, and we are thankful that it harmed us not. These thoughts, being emanations from the Spirit of God, they will remain stored up for a day of need, they will return just at the right moment. They will stand at the gate of heaven, and will open it, even though we may not yet be able to enter in; yet may some ministrant issue forth summoned by the silent voice of a long-forgotten memory, or the revival of a past feeling conveyed in the sweet breath of a half-withered flower that a seeming chance has cast in our way. A ray of light penetrates into a darkened chamber, no one may see through what chink it enters. So come man's thoughts, —who shall say what thought shall come next, or what object the eye shall next rest on? What event of life will stamp the coming morrow with a permanent significance? Who that shall say what may be the consequence of that morrow's dawn,—what long passed memories may be awakened,—what dark forebodings stilled, or what bright prospects opened?

The Scripture does not say, "I will refine whosoever is willing to be refined," but "He is a refiner of silver;" and as the silver has no will of its own in the matter of its refinement, so neither have men, for they know not that they need purification, that they should seek the means of it.

My brother, live not in the silent chamber of death. Mourn not for the days that are past;—they came as an outbirth from that which shall remain for ever; their work is done, and is treasured up in the storehouse of eternity. Other days are passing now, and immortal spirits are passing away, and their memory is as a pleasant melody.

Pleasant fancies are readily awakened, and dark thoughts sink to rest. How is it with you? and how with you? Each one will give a different reply, and modesty will lower the head and answer nothing; but ONE hears that which no language can convey in thought or in word. He will hear as no man or angel can. The mortal ear hears not His voice. The immortal ear is open when the mortal organ is alone conscious, or the natural ear may be made the key by means of which the chamber of the spirit is unlocked. Both hold near and intimate relations. When the natural ear transmits no harmony to the soul, then must that inner sense be closed; but it still exists, and may be opened by the atmospheres of heaven.

FINIS.

www.ingramcontent.com/pod-product-compliance
Lightning Source LLC
Chambersburg PA
CBHW031348230426
43670CB00006B/468